THE DEBT FREE DIVA
FROM SELF WORTH TO NET WORTH

Dee Dee Sung

The Sung Group Inc
Copyright 2003 by Dee Dee Sung
All rights reserved. Printed in Canada. No part
of this book may be used or reproduced without
written permission. For information contact
The Sung Group Inc at 1-888-313-9604

ISBN: 0-9734055-0-3

Attention: Businesses and schools

Books are available at quantity discounts with
bulk purchases for business, sales promotional or
educational use. For information, contact
The Sung Group Inc at 1-888-313-9604
www.debtfreediva.com

Cover: Chick Rice
Book Design: Lesley Wright

Dedication

To Mum

Your indomitable spirit is with me always,

I love you…

TABLE OF CONTENTS

Introduction • *The Coin* 3
Chapter 1 • *Money Mirror* 7
Chapter 2 • *Be Willing* 17
Chapter 3 • *Have a Dream* 31
Chapter 4 • *Dreams in Motion* 47
Chapter 5 • *Balancing Act* 57
Chapter 6 • *Worthy and Wonderful* 67
Chapter 7 • *Progress, Not Perfection* 81
Chapter 8 • *Get Real* 91
Chapter 9 • *Diva Debt in Perspective* 101
Chapter 10 • *Fund the Dream* 111
Chapter 11 • *Order Order* 123
Chapter 12 • *It Takes Two* 139
Chapter 13 • *Work, Work, Work* 151
Chapter 14 • *A Change of Scenery* 161
Chapter 15 • *Live the Dream* 171
Acknowledgements 181

INTRODUCTION

As a teenager and young adult I never really thought about money. I guess it was just always there for me – my parents had more than enough to go around and I was always given more than my share. As I got older I knew that I was fortunate, but I didn't know that my relationship to money was not a healthy one. My parents gave me everything I wanted – and money started to represent an expression of love. As I reached my late 20's suddenly the checks stopped coming. I was working and out on my own – I was now responsible for myself. And I was responsible for my money.

I spent the next several years in and out of debt, in and out of relationships and in and out of jobs. I realized that my unhealthy relationship to money had affected so many other areas of my life that I had to do something. I had to heal that relationship, but how?

I started to really ponder how I felt in the pit of my stomach and the thoughts that were racing through my head, when I was late yet again on my credit card payments. Or the embarrassment and shame that came from not being able to pay back a friend. If money represented love, was I now unlovable? That's when I knew that I had to heal myself from within and I started the process. The process you are about to experience in this book.

The combination of my personal experience and my background in finance and psychology was what got me started – but it was the heart-breaking stories of hundreds of women I spoke with that provided the inspiration to write *The Debt Free Diva – From Self Worth to Net Worth*.

I've learned from these conversations that you can't always judge a book by its cover. One woman I met had a high profile job with a six-figure income. She was living beyond her means by portraying an affluent lifestyle – she purchased the best of everything – the house, the car, the clothes. She seemed to walk the walk and definitely talked the talk like she had everything together, but she was thousands of dollars in debt and it was eating her up inside. Another woman had a substantial nest egg set aside, was comfortable and at peace with herself – on a $22,000 income. Many women weren't in financial trouble, but something was missing and they weren't at peace. Sometimes becoming aware of a problem and making a small change can make all the difference in the world. And we can become aware by working on ourselves from the inside out.

Women with financial problems come in all shapes and sizes – I could never tell who was at peace and who was in trouble by looking at them. We needed to talk. The common thread that ran through most of the stories I heard revolved around fear – the fear of not thinking they had enough, would ever have enough or were simply *not* enough with respect to their sense of self worth. This was further confirmation that I needed to write a book that addressed our money issues from within. When we can determine why we do the things we do, there is greater opportunity for change.

People always ask me why I decided to focus on women. Men and women communicate differently and they solve problems differently. As a woman who has felt the pain, fear and stress of financial burdens, I feel that the writing of this book was my true calling. My purpose and passion is to help other women reinvent their relationship to money in a positive way. More importantly, nine out of ten women will at some time in their lives be solely responsible for their own finances. Now is the time – more than ever – that the message of reinventing your self worth in order to increase your net worth be made available. Although this book was written with Divas in mind, it can also help the Dudes in your life!

INTRODUCTION

While in the midst of writing this book, I came across an ancient Chinese coin that seemed to instantly crystallize my thoughts. The coin struck me as an obvious representation of money, but it was the square hole in the center that really spoke to me. As I looked inside this *window*, I realized that I was *looking through money*. I thought it was a perfect symbol of my many messages in this book. The window represents what is behind and within money – good and bad. When we look *through* our relationship to money at ourselves, we have the capability to explore and gain understanding and insight into our level of self worth and ultimately our net worth. As we move from self worth to net worth, we are constantly looking at ourselves. The meaning of the coin will become clear to you too – as you read through the book and complete the exercises. The purpose of writing this book is to show you that a Debt Free Diva experiences freedom in every area of her life and that it is ultimately one's emotional debt that creates unwanted, financial debt. You will soon realize that it's not about the money. Within that realization lies the key to your freedom!

My wish is that you will want to re-read this book over and over throughout your journey. And that at anytime, whatever page you open up to – the passage you were meant to read is staring you in the face. Each chapter includes one affirmation that I call *Diva Speak* as the basis for the information and exercises in that chapter. *The Debt Free Diva* is formatted to guide you through the process of reinventing your relationship to money in a systematic way – while enjoying the ride in the process.

As a true *Debt Free Diva* – here are my intentions for you:
- To be willing to see your relationship to money from a new perspective – your *true* perspective.
- To be open to telling the truth about your current relationship to money so that you can take positive steps.
- To become *your* own dream maker.
- To be willing to track your expenses and record your progress each day for 90 days.
- To become capable of attaining your money goals.
- To become confident in knowing that you have all the time and money you need to feel secure and live your dreams.
- To be abundant in your self worth and your net worth.
- To be able to handle your money with E.A.S.E and always have money available.
- To be responsible with your debt and keep it in perspective.
- To be open and receptive to learning the basics of investing.
- To be the *CEO* in all areas of your financial life – *Creating Extraordinary Outcomes*.
- To be clear and concise in your communication about money.
- To be open and receptive to creating a work environment that honors who you are.
- To be flexible with financial changes in your life and to handle them with confidence and ease.

I feel that the support of others is so helpful as we take this journey to create a positive relationship to money. Please log on and stay tuned to my web-site at **www.debtfreediva.com**. I would also love to hear from you, so e-mail me with your progress and stories. My goal is to create a community of Debt Free Divas so we all have someone to learn from and someone to lean on. Share your fears, your challenges, and your victories with others so we can all help each other. Every one of you deserves to live the life you dream of!

Have a fantastic journey.

CHAPTER 1
MONEY MIRROR

"We don't see things as they are, we see things as we are."

Anais Nin

CHAPTER 1 • MONEY MIRROR

DIVA SPEAK:
I am open to telling the truth about my current relationship to money so that I can take positive steps.

Money affects every area of our lives. You may not think of dollars and cents as something with which you hold a *relationship*, but like it or not, you do. Imagine your interactions with money as a dance. If your partner is too tall or too short, too wild or aloof, the dance is torturous and out of step. The more you learn about your partner, the more you learn to spin and turn in time with the rhythms of your income, outlay and attitudes towards money, the more *flow* enters into your life. Believe it or not, money is here to supply you with the means to live your dreams. The paradox is that money – or more accurately, the lack of money – prevents most people from living the life they want. The first step to getting your money life in order is to understand your relationship to it.

We're all regular about checking the mirror to see if our hair, our tie or our hemline is in proper place; this book will teach you to do the same with your finances, so we begin with a good look into the money mirror. Don't be afraid! It's not a dark dungeon – it is, instead, a bright and shiny portal to a new world, one you will find increasingly easier to enter as you move through the practices presented in this book. So put a smile on your face, take a deep breath, and turn your eyes inside.

How do you feel when the subject of money surfaces? When you pay your bills, do your banking or plop down cold, hard cash, what emotions or thoughts arise?

WHAT IS MONEY?

Money represents different things to different people. As we move through this book, you'll probably be surprised at some of the money attitudes, beliefs and behaviors you never *consciously* knew you held. From a factual perspective, money possesses the following characteristics:

- Money is life energy – a means of exchange for goods and services.
- Money in and of itself has no value – our experiences with it determine the value we place upon it.
- Money can be both master and servant – it is up to us to choose which role it will play in our lives.
- Money is a necessity – we all need it to exist, so it's important that our relationship to it is healthy.
- Money is a taboo subject in our society – an emotionally charged topic not readily or openly discussed. In fact, there's not a single topic, *including* sex, which is so stringently avoided in public. Ironically, it's the unwillingness to openly discuss it that creates and maintains the mystery.

What does money mean to you? Some people believe it is a measure of success while others think of it simply as a form of exchange for goods and services. Is it Love? Power? Control? Security? Is it a Weapon or a Shield?

At different times in my life, money has represented love, power, acceptance or self worth. Today, I see money as a *tool* to *serve me* in attaining my goals and dreams! As I become more in tune with the fact that money is here to serve me rather than a means by which I can gain acceptance in the world, I create a new perspective, a new relationship to finances. There's far less emotional charge around it now.

Let's get into the nitty-gritty and uncover the deep-seeded beliefs that lie at the basis of *your* relationship to money.

To make this process work for you, it's important to be willing to *tell the truth*. No one will see your work in this book unless you choose to share it, so hunker down and decide to be totally honest with yourself. Knowing what you write is for your eyes only, grab a "green-light" attitude and complete the following sentence:

To me, money represents...

_____

_____

MONEY MYTHS

What is a Myth?
A myth is a story or belief held by a culture or group of people, a common "truth," widely accepted and often carrying a meaning of it's own. George Washington felled a cherry tree and said "I cannot tell a lie" – True or False? It never really happened, but the story is dear to American hearts because it represents qualities inherent to our national ideals – honesty and integrity. Money myths are equally ingrained in our thoughts and lives, and it is our attachment to them that often makes it impossible for us to come to positive financial decisions.

We can *literally* "buy into" a myth, make it our "story," and allow the myth to determine the habits and beliefs we develop about money. They become so automatic we don't even realize we subscribe to them. In order to reinvent our relationship to money, we must first become *aware* of the *money myths* we finance, and how they shape our attitudes and behaviors. If you want to know what drives you to act, start paying attention to the words you use and the thoughts you hold concerning money. As you'll soon discover, your thoughts form your beliefs, which form your reality.

Consider the following list of common money myths. Check the ones that apply to you, and add any extras that you say to others or think to yourself. From now on, pay close attention to when and how often you use them and in what context. Remember, awareness of your current patterns and habits is the key to making the changes you desire in your relationship to money.

Here we go…
- Money is the root of all evil.
- It takes money to make money.
- Once you're in debt, you can never get out.
- Budgeting is impossible.
- Investing is for the rich.
- The rich get richer and the poor get poorer.
- Rich people are snobs.
- She's filthy rich.
- He's dirt poor.
- It's impossible to make ends meet on my salary.
- When I have X number of dollars, I'll be happy.

Fill in a few sayings about money that you've said or heard from others:

_____

_____

_____

What emotions or physical sensations did you experience as you considered each myth?

_____

_____

_____

Which ones have you bought into? How have they served you?

_____

_____

_____

Well done! Being aware of the Money Myths that you've financed over the years is a very important step. Have any of them played a *positive* role in your relationship to money?

MONEY PERSONALITIES

Just as we individually fall into basic psychological types – such as introvert/extrovert – in our overall behaviors, we also function through a spectrum of six money personalities, to which we will refer throughout this book. Most of us vacillate between types from time to time, so the one you pick today may be different from the one that fits next week. Have some fun with this! I certainly did, in picking the names and creating their stories!

- **Spenderella** and **Spenderfella** are well dressed, and spend money mindlessly, on anything and everything. Buying makes them feel good, so they shop when they're happy, shop when they're sad, shop when they're anxious, depressed or just plain bored. "Spend, spend, spend" is their mantra!
- **Lackwanno** and **Lackwanna** are always just one day short of being broke and believe there is never enough – of anything, including money. Even when the tank is full, they seem to be running on empty.

- **Hoardesia** and **Hoardesio** hoard their money and don't find any pleasure in the present moment. When they do spend, it's on *quantity* instead of *quality*. They are afraid of not having enough down the road so they stockpile *stuff* today in order to assure security tomorrow. They can't bear to part with anything – including their money.
- **Feartensio** and **Feartensia** are afraid of the past, afraid of the present and totally terrified of the future. They live in the belief that there wasn't enough, isn't enough and never will be enough, and changes would only make things worse.
- **Oblivia** and **Oblivio** basically ignore anything having to do with money. They don't know, don't want to know and don't care about money – and they question why they're in a *money mess*. They say things like "Money's not important to me" in order to avoid admitting their lack of awareness and control.
- **Prospero** and **Prospera** are comfortable and in flow with money. They have the ideal outlook and know that money is here to serve them. They have faith that there will always be plenty of money, and know that there is always money coming in. They spend, save, give back and enjoy every dollar they have. They are responsible, and realize that you don't need lots of money to be prosperous. They are wealthy within, which in turn generates an outer demonstration of prosperity.

Well, how did you do? What style or combination of styles do you think fits you?

Do you want to change?

Which of our characters do you want to manifest in your relationship with money?

If you're a little Spenderella today, a little Feartensio next week and a little Prospera every other Tuesday it's OK. Becoming aware of our money personality is important for us as individuals, but there is also a big picture context here, as people who come together in relationships rarely have the same money personalities. When you say *stop* and your partner says *go*, things can get dicey. We'll talk more about money personalities in relationships in a later chapter.

There are three distinct money styles, incorporating all of the characters we've introduced:
1) Live for today, forget about tomorrow (usually Spenderella or Oblivio.)
2) Live for tomorrow, forget today (usually Feartensia, Hoardesio, or Lackwanna.)
3) Live for today and live for tomorrow (usually Prospero.)

MONEY QUIZ

Much of what shapes your relationship to money is determined by your level of awareness around your habits of spending, saving and investing. Take the following money quiz and be truthful. In order to create positive, lasting change, it's important to know where you're starting.

1) I have thought a lot about my spending habits and relationship to money and know that I need to change in order to create the relationship that I want.
    True   False
2) I am willing to learn the steps to create positive and lasting change with my relationship to money.
    True   False
3) I am tired of always feeling like I don't have enough money.
    True   False
4) I accept the idea that I can reinvent my relationship to money by taking some basic steps.
    True   False
5) I want to improve my relationship to money because I deserve it.
    True   False
6) Reinventing my relationship to money will clear up other problems in my life.
    True   False
7) I am willing and able to take these steps no matter how uncomfortable I feel.
    True   False
8) I feel I'm behind in saving for my future and it's too late to save enough.
    True   False

9) I often fall off track when starting something new and can't get motivated to start up again.
True   False
10) When I'm feeling stressed, I go shopping.
True   False
11) I often spend money I don't have in order to feel better about myself.
True   False
12) I'm embarrassed about my net worth and often compare myself to others who seem to have more.
True   False
13) My *self* worth is tied to my *net* worth.
True   False
14) I don't like discussing money because I don't know enough about how to handle it.
True   False

Scoring: If you answered *true* to any of these questions, you're ready to learn through this book. It is clear that your intention to improve your relationship to money is important to you. Being willing to tell the truth and being willing to change will enable you to find success with this self-study process. If answering these questions truthfully made you cringe – you're not alone! Many people who have been successful with the materials in this book have had similar feelings in the beginning. The most important thing is to be aware of where you are today and be willing to take positive action.

So what have you learned from looking in the *Money Mirror?* Are you cringing, or laughing? Are you ready to move into a new, invigorating way of relating to and functioning with your finances? Now that you've come this far, it's time to take the next step, and all it takes is for you to be *willing* to make a choice, and make a change.

Let's get started…

CHAPTER 2
BE WILLING

"Character – the willingness to accept responsibility for one's own life – is the source from which self-respect springs."

Joan Didion

CHAPTER 2 • BE WILLING

DIVA SPEAK:
I am willing to see my relationship to money from a new perspective – my true perspective.

The greatest joy in **Spenderella's** life was the hours she filled shopping for the perfect dress, the perfect shoes, the perfect chair, the perfect desk. Fulfillment came from a buying spree, followed by monumental dread when the bills arrived each month. Spenderella believed she would never get out of her mountain of debt, so she kept shopping, and couldn't come to grips with the cycle of her habits. One day her friend Prospera told her of the life she once lived, a life identical to Spenderella's, and how she had come to change her habits and her name. Prospera suggested there was equal fulfillment in paying off her debt and structuring a reasonable spending plan. She offered to help create a strategy. Spenderella took a good, hard look at her finances and habits, and committed to sticking to her plan. Within a few months the tidal wave of bills began to subside. She felt energized, in control and excited to expand her plan to other financial areas – a great relief and change from the highs and lows she experienced before!

Our adventure through the money mirror and into the journey of becoming debt-free starts with a single word. *Willingness.* A simple word, certainly, but not necessarily a simple task. Willingness empowers you to create positive and lasting change in your relationship to money and everything else in your life. But what does it really mean to *be willing?* It means being excited and open to new experiences, new thoughts, new behaviors. It means looking through the ancient Chinese coin. Willingness is a *choice*. It means choosing to consider and make change not because you *have to* but because you acknowledge the benefit that choice will bring to you, all the while being conscious that before the benefit comes, there will be challenges. When we go along with the crowd in order to *be* a part of the crowd, that's not willingness – that's resignation. We gain personal freedom the moment we choose to approach even the most difficult challenge of our lives with a sense of adventure and excitement. When you are willing and open to change, all the pieces will come into place, one adventurous step at a time.

- Be willing to do what *you* really want in life, rather than what you believe is expected of you, or what everyone else seems to be doing.
- Be willing to stop "renting a lifestyle," trying to maintain an image that isn't the *real* you.
- Be willing to *tell the truth.*

CHANGE IN YOUR LIFE = CHANGE IN YOUR POCKET
If you can change your mind, you can change your money.
Change means progress, *not* perfection. Change means stepping into a process – you can't just close your eyes, click your heels and say "There's no place like financial freedom" and expect your money woes to disappear down a yellow brick road. But you can pull back the curtain that masks your inner Oz, turn on your brain and your heart, and fill them both with courage. The choice to do so is the harbinger of *willingness* – the choice to take that first, tentative step. That is the turning point, the fork in the road – the choice between *All or Nothing* on the one hand, and *Something is Better Than Nothing* on the other. To change your mind is to shift your perception, which will in turn change your reality with money.

We've all had experiences that carry the All-or-Nothing dynamic. You do well on a diet for a while, cheat "just a little" by eating a slice of chocolate cake, and then, as if you were faced with the-end-of-the-world-is-NOW, tell yourself "I've blown it! Why bother to continue? I may as well eat a quart of ice cream." You're going to get off track in reinventing your relationship to money – and that's OK. Thomas Edison created several thousand versions of the light bulb before he got to the one that worked. When you fall down, acknowledge it, wiggle a bit to shake off the dust, and get right back on track.

You're probably thinking "that's easy for you to say, hard for me to do!" and, I have no doubt that up to now that was true. But here's a new truth: You can do it all with *ease* – that is, with E.A.S.E.

THE E.A.S.E. APPROACH

How many times have you thought or said Life is Hard?

It's a myth.

Do you say *Life is Hard* when the topic of money is raised? If you answered *"Yes,"* thank you for telling the truth.

There is little motivation to change when everything feels hard and overwhelming, but the good news is that life doesn't *have to* be hard. Unbelievable as it may seem to you right now, we make choices as to how we view life and the situations that occur in our lives. We may not choose the circumstances, but we always choose the way we react or respond to them. Life happens, things happen that we haven't anticipated, and often we have a financial mess on our hands that we would like to forget. We've all used the standard excuses at one time or another, excuses like:

- I don't make enough money
- I was left with this financial mess
- I lost my job
- I'm a compulsive spender
- My spouse spends money like water through a sieve.

The "it's not my fault" list is endless, debilitating and counterproductive. Right here, right now, write down all the excuses you can think of for your current financial state. When you're done, take a good look at the list, and make a choice to let all those excuses go. Then rip that paper into shreds and dump it in the trash – or burn it, or go outside and toss it to the wind, because right here and right now, you're beginning to approach your relationship to money with grace, dignity, and E.A.S.E. – a process that is simple to understand and simple to use. The key is to be willing to incorporate all four steps into your life.

Education: Throughout this book, I will direct you to websites and other resources that will provide the basic financial knowledge you need to educate yourself. Make your education an adventure, not a chore. You may feel, in the beginning, that you've opened Pandora's proverbial box and now there's a thousand financial terms and two hundred gnats of confusing advice swarming around your overstuffed head. Find a way to make it fun, because when you get to the bottom of Pandora's box, there is a great and glorious gem. Make your education a treasure hunt, and know that the gem is worth having. And you are worthy of having the gem – a life of financial prosperity and abundance.

Action: Take one small step at a time. The only way you will ever fail in this book is if you choose to do nothing with it. Fear of failure and fear of success are virtually the same – we're scared to try and we're scared to take action! A child cannot run without learning to walk, cannot walk without learning to crawl, cannot crawl without stretching and testing, one muscle movement at a time. These incremental steps turn into monumental progress. The key is to *start* – from there, each step is easier. Before you know it, you'll be waving your financial statements around as if they were Olympic gold.

Support: We've all said it at one time or another – "I got myself into this mess, now I'd better get myself out." That's a Catch-22! You got yourself into the mess, what makes you think you can get yourself out of it on your own? It's hard to ask for help. For some reason, we believe that we're supposed to *know it all* and have all the answers, that by the time we reach adulthood we should be able to handle all of life's twists and turns with the skill of a professional racecar driver. The truth is, when it comes to money most of us are still cruising around in a push-cart, waiting for a strong wind to fill our ragged sails. Be willing to admit that you don't know it all. Acknowledge how quick *you* are to lend a hand to others, and be willing to ask for guidance and assistance. Support is critical if you're committed to improving and reinventing your relationship to money, so crumble up that "I can do it myself" attitude and toss it away. Talk to a financially-sound friend or family member you respect, subscribe to a money magazine, or join the Debt Free Diva Community on the Internet. Most people love to help, and support is all around you – be willing to reach out.

Energize: Once you've made a positive change, once you've seen the first light of success and are living in the delight of feeling good about yourself, take the next step. Energize yourself further by helping someone else. That friend who scoffed at your efforts to make positive changes? They fear the movement in your life because it brings to light the changes they need to make in their own. They'd rather stay stuck in a behavior that doesn't serve them because the fear of change is too great; your success only heightens their own sense of failure. Make your changes anyway, and be a support to them when they gather their courage down the road. There's always someone who will benefit from your experience. And there's no greater reward, nothing more empowering, than helping someone else reinvent their relationship to money.

Relax in your chair and read through the following instructions. Once you understand the process, close your eyes, jump inside yourself, and see what happens.

- Imagine tracking your expenses, or keeping your checkbook balanced, or making some other change in the way you interact with your money.
- If you just felt anxious – it's OK. It is common to immediately feel stressed or out of control because the space between a highly-ingrained habit and a new, desired behavior – *the gap* – is an uncharted, limitless place. It's scary because we have no concept of control or boundaries when we are there.
- Now take a deep breath, and imagine that the change you desire has already taken place, and it happened easily and effortlessly.
- How do you *feel*?

It's important to really feel our desired change on the inside. Thinking and seeing the change is not enough since the voice of doubt will eventually creep in. Feeling creates emotion, emotion creates energy and energy creates results.

The extent of your stress or your peaceful empowerment in this exercise is a choice. Remember that all things are possible if you are truly willing. As we go through this book continue to see and feel yourself exhibiting new, positive and proactive behaviors. Remember the story of the cab driver who was asked "how do you get to Carnegie Hall?" His response was "practice, practice, practice." When you maintain a consistent practice of visualizing yourself living your desired *life with ease*, your subconscious mind brings them and the circumstances that promote them to three-dimensional reality. I'll go into this in more depth later; for now, be willing to imagine, and have some fun with it

– dress yourself up, give yourself airs, surround yourself with your wildest dreams. Then be ready to see them come to life.

WILLINGNESS QUESTIONNAIRE

Even one "yes" is enough. Be honest with yourself, and be willing to honor yourself for your honesty.

1) Am I willing to be open to thinking about money in a new way?
2) Am I willing to let go of past perceptions and mistakes I have made with money?
3) Am I willing to do whatever it takes to create a positive relationship to money?
4) Am I willing to do it with E.A.S.E.?

Good Job! The next page is a personal contract, which will serve as a constant reminder of the commitment you have made to yourself. Copy it and sign it – then hang it on your bathroom mirror, tape it to the wall next to your bed, or put it someplace else where you, and your subconscious mind, will see it and read it every day, with a smile on your face, knowing you are on a road of your own choosing that will bring you closer to your dreams. After you've signed the contract and hung it in a prominent place, we'll move on to your money biography.

PERSONAL CONTRACT

This is a personal contract I have made with myself, to take the steps necessary to reinvent my relationship to money.

I, (NAME) _____
agree to the following:

1) I will be open to new ways of creating positive and lasting change in my life.
2) I agree to be willing to complete each section of this course no matter how uncomfortable I may feel.
3) I will suspend my current perceptions of what I believe to be true about money.
4) I will journey through this course seeking progress, not perfection.
5) I will complete this course using the E.A.S.E. approach to learning.

I acknowledge that it is possible to create positive and lasting change in my relationship to money. The past is gone, and has no hold on me. From this day forward, I am willing to forgive myself for past mistakes and move forward creating all the time and money I need to live my dreams!

Signed _____

Dated _____

MONEY BIOGRAPHY

By the time we head off to elementary school, our primary role models – usually our parents – have taught us a great deal. We know how to tie our shoes, brush our teeth, say *please* and *thank you*. We've also been taught, through direct statements, familial attitudes, and situational behaviors, many ways of participating in society that are directly related to the money personalities with which we function through puberty and into adulthood. Your experiences with family money myths and habits may be totally different than those of the kid next door, but much like a collection of music CD's, most are variations on common themes.

Experiences that occurred in such a distant part of your past that you have no memory of them still have significant, lasting impact on your life. Sometimes we don't even know what we do or don't know! Your *Money Biography* will help to identify the thoughts and attitudes about finances that were formed early in your life, the events that caused them, and the impact they have had on your relationship with money. Standing face-to-face with the timeline of your money beliefs allows you to take the first plunge into the pool of transformation without feeling you are standing high above the water on a shaky diving board.

As kids, we assumed our parents knew *everything* about money. We assumed they knew *everything* about *everything*. In many cases, we were wrong. How much do you know about the way money was handled in your childhood home? Did one parent control all the finances? Was there always enough, or never enough? Were your parents generous or stringent with money? Did money represent power or love in your family?

Few of us were given formal training in money management as children; thankfully, it's never too late to learn! Knowing that you or the people around you would have *done* better if they *knew* better brings a willful act of forgiveness, a release from the energy drain and weight of constantly looking over our shoulder to pass blame on our past for the conditions of our present – a practice that prevents us from moving forward.

Think back through your life and recall events that may have impacted your relationship to money. Did your father lose his job? Did your mother tell you that your family couldn't afford something you desperately wanted? Did you hear derogatory comments about rich people or poor people? Did you use money and things as a way to get what you wanted? Did you or your family use money to impress others? Our past experiences create our current reality. Spend some time on this, think hard and try to remember as much detail as you can. Then look at the way events or beliefs that came from your past still play out in your life today.

Time	Event	Impact
Age 10 and under	_____	_____
Age 11-20	_____	_____
Age 21-30	_____	_____
Age 31-40	_____	_____
Age 41-50	_____	_____
Age 51 and over	_____	_____

Are you surprised at some of the memories that came forward for you in this exercise? When we see all the events that impacted our relationship to money on one page, it can help us make sense of our current financial condition.

Revisit this exercise frequently over the next few weeks and include additional events that come to mind. As you begin to recall and understand the ingredients that have gone into your money relationship, the correlation between your past and present attitudes will become clearer. Remember, this is a process of discovery, not finding ways to beat yourself up for past mistakes and events.

When you're finished, take a break and clear your mind. You've done a lot of mental processing and may feel tired. Great work!

The process of letting go of the past is crucial to moving forward. Hanging onto the past creates excuses; keep us feeling down and in a negative frame of mind. Letting go gives us a new perspective that is important in creating positive change.

FIRST STEPS COLLAGE

Muscles grow and stay strong when they are exercised regularly; your "money muscle" needs exercise, too, and we often have to sneak in the back door to see what's really going on in the kitchen. The next exercise may appear frivolous to you at first, but by the time we are finished with this book, it's impact will be clear to you. With the next exercise, I'm asking you to stretch your mind and your imagination to take a "back-door" approach.

You will be creating a collage, also known as a storyboard, that represents your current attitudes and beliefs about money. Think of it as a way to download your thoughts.

Here's what you'll need:
1) A large piece of poster board
2) Glue stick
3) Scissors
4) Colored pens or markers
5) Magazines
6) Catalogs
7) Bank Statements
8) Credit Card Statements
9) Cancelled or NSF Checks

If your mind is already telling you reasons why you shouldn't do this exercise, thank it for sharing and continue on! I can hear it now... "It's too much trouble...don't bother!" Just remember for a moment how much you loved arts and crafts in elementary school, how much time you spent at the kitchen table with plastic scissors, construction paper and Elmer's glue, and the absolute pride you felt when mom taped your chubby-fingered equivalent of the Mona Lisa on the refrigerator door. Get your head in that space and make your collage an equally worthy piece of art!

Your storyboard is simply a snapshot in time, one of those "Kodak Moments" that will help you to realize that change is possible. Think about those "before and after" photos you see in weight-loss product ads – that's what you're doing here – creating the "before" picture. When you reach your financial goal you'll be totally excited by the changes that took place, and totally proud to know that you were responsible for the transformation.

Most people take one or two hours of uninterrupted time to complete the collage, but there is no prescribed time limit – if you need two or three sittings to complete your storyboard, don't get discouraged. Do what works for you, but do it!

Browse through magazines and catalogs, cutting out anything that may represent your feelings about money. There are no rights or wrongs – let your mind wander and clip anything that triggers a thought or pulls an emotion, but stay relaxed. Remember that this is not a representation of *who* you are, but is, instead, representative of *where* you are at this moment. Be sure to tell the truth, and remember that this collage is for *your eyes only*, at least for the duration of this course. Pile up your clippings with your bank statements or credit card statements and start gluing images to your board. Write down any negative self-talk that floods your brain – you might, for example, find yourself thinking "This bill will take me *forever* to pay off." Write it on the storyboard, next to or underneath that credit card statement. Don't force associations or emotions – do what comes naturally. When you've finished your collage, display it in a place where only you will be able to see it. We'll be returning to it soon.

Your myths, personality, habits, patterns and biography are all key ingredients of your money story. When your car grows old and stops running, it's time to get a new one. The same is true for your story, and you can trade your money story in for something better just as easily as you said goodbye to that rusty sedan you inherited as a teenager. You'll be using transformational tools throughout this book and beyond, that will call you to put the "I" factor into action – an acknowledgement that *you* are the key player in reinventing your relationship to money. You are called to make agreements with yourself, which you may feel like breaking from time to time. When you do, *I* encourage you to continue as if you didn't miss a beat. I did it, and so can you. The agreements are:

I am willing to change
I am able to change
I deserve to change
I am worthy of change

Repeat them often. Make them your mantra. Let them become a song that replaces negative chatter in your head. Above all, feel what it's like to have made the desired changes – feel it in every cell of your body. Practice these feelings in 15-second increments and take note of your energy levels. By repeating these throughout the day, you'll start to energize your desires into reality. Remember, it's your choice whether to focus on the positive or dwell in the negative. The place where you direct your attention will be the place that will come into existence for you.

Coupled with the contract you've made, the insight you've gained from your money biography and your starting point collage, the agreements will bolster your resolve and work within your subconscious mind to move you toward the subject of our next chapter – defining and fulfilling your dreams.

CHAPTER 3
HAVE A DREAM

"The future belongs to those who believe in the beauty of their dream."

Eleanor Roosevelt

CHAPTER 3 • HAVE A DREAM

DIVA SPEAK:
I am my own dream weaver.

Lackwanna's burning desire was a year-end vacation in a tropical locale, far away from icy roads and slippery schedules. Believing her salary was too small to manage saving $3,000 in the ten months before her hoped-for departure, Lackwanna heaved a mighty sigh, and said "maybe next year," full of resignation and disappointment. One day, her friend Prospero told her the story of how he purchased his new home. "I didn't know how I would ever come up with the money for a down payment, but I did know that if I kept believing the money would come, it would happen," he said. "Every day I imagined myself writing that check and receiving the keys to my new home. Everyday I told myself that somehow it would happen, and it did." Prospero offered to help Lackwanna create an affirmation that would help her hold her dream in her heart and mind in a positive, fun way. Lackwanna began to remind herself daily that she was open to the abundant resources available to her in making her trip happen. She imagined herself strolling the beach, sipping exotic drinks with pink umbrella stir-sticks, and dancing to island music underneath a big, red banner that said "Paid in Full." There were moments, and even days, when repeating the affirmation and visualization were difficult, but she persisted. A few months before her departure date, Lackwanna received an unexpected tax refund, sold an old desk in her basement to an antique dealer, and found she had made an error in balancing her checkbook that raised her balance by several hundred dollars. By the time she headed for the airport, Lackwanna even had enough money to afford a new swimsuit, and treat herself to dinner at a five-star restaurant on the island. She had become her own dream-weaver.

DREAMS

Dreams are created in the space between your head and your heart. Desires and emotions well up from your heart, and your head sets about bringing them to reality. Head and Heart must be able to talk to each other, to work as a team, if you are ever to have the Will to manifest your dreams. Your heart, your desires and your emotions create your dreams. Imagine you have a best friend on the opposite side of the world, and the two of you plan to meet somewhere in between. Anticipation is high, but something goes awry – he flew to Birmingham, Alabama – you flew to Birmingham, England.

What do you *really* want out of life when it comes to money? How can you achieve your goals and dreams if you don't know what they are? For many of us, the dreams we seek are vague and shadowy – idyllic images that have no foundation or structure. So you say "I want to have a million dollars." That's what comes out of your mouth – this arbitrary dollar amount – but in your heart is a longing to set up a foundation for abandoned children, or send you grandchildren to college, or take a cruise on the QE2. There is lack of communication, and lack of clarity between your head and your heart.

We need to question our dreams. We need to ask "Why is this dream important to me?" We need to put ourselves into the dream so deeply that we can see it, feel it, taste it and smell it when we imagine it – and then ask "Is this what I *really* want, and why?" Does this dream really represent something you *want*, or does it stem from your money biography or myth? How will your life be when you reach that goal, and what are the reasons you want it to be the way you imagine it?

Take a look at the diagram below:

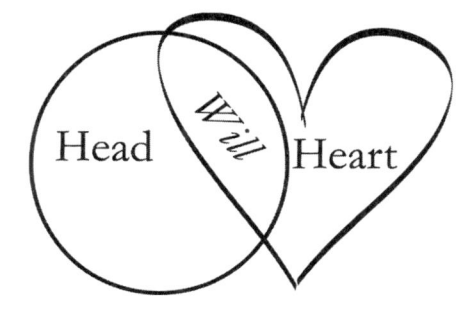

```
    Head  Will  Heart
```

We need to energize the space where head and heart overlap – this is where Will resides. This is the land of total synergy; when it is activated, realizing your goals and dreams becomes the most natural thing to do. If our head and heart are at odds with each other, our Will has no clear direction to follow.

FEELINGS

If the head is what we think and the heart is what we know, where do feelings come in? I like to think of feelings as the "current," or the "static electricity" that connects the head and heart. A positive feeling brings the two together in a way that propels us toward our dreams. On the other hand, a negative feeling or "current" usually moves us away from our dreams or keeps us stuck in a rut. Positive feelings bring the energy and the emotion to our lives and keep us motivated to keep striving for what we really want.

CREATING THE DESIRES OF OUR HEARTS

Creating is a very powerful word. When we describe someone as *creative*, what do we mean? I first think of artists, those who can paint a masterpiece from a blank canvas or someone who can compose a beautiful song from a group of musical notes on a piano. Let's think of creating the desires of our hearts in the same way – a process that will bring us our *masterpiece*.

Creating a true masterpiece requires patience, commitment, discipline and sacrifice. It's been said that good things come to those who wait. I'm not talking about sitting around and actually *waiting*. I'm talking about having the *patience* to have the clarity in our hearts, minds and feelings to know which way to venture. Once we're clear, we need to have the patience to know that the people, events and circumstances will come together to give us what we need. Commitment, discipline and sacrifice can all have negative connotations. But staying true to our desires, never waffling, and being willing to do whatever it takes keeps the creative process in motion.

It's like baking a cake. We need all of the ingredients to create the ultimate desires of our hearts.

VALUES

Enjoying the journey is just as important as reaching the destination; have fun with your dreams and your analysis of them. Every question you ask brings you one step closer to clarity, one step closer to being able to manifest your dream, and brings you face-to-face with a critical aspect of your reasons – your values.

What is most important to you? Is it important to send your kids to college? Is it important to travel the world, or own a home? Have a closet full of fashionable clothes? Is it important to frequent fine restaurants? Go to the movies or the opera?

What has value in your life? You may discover that the things you really value are left unfunded because you are spending mindlessly on items that have no long-lasting importance in your life.

It's easy to get caught up in the latest fad, or the image you think you need to project. Consider *your* values, not your neighbor's.

What is valuable in your life right now? Take stock of the things you are grateful for today. I've made this a part of my daily ritual, and it has changed my outlook and perspective dramatically. It's a simple task – each morning I write down three things in my life for which I am grateful. When I wake up feeling preoccupied and less than excited about the day, my gratitude ritual changes the vibration – changes the energy around me, because my focus has shifted from what I *want* to what I already *have*. When we're filled with the feeling of gratitude we feel invincible. Our possibilities are endless. A daily gratitude *recital* opens space for more and more prosperity, insight and creativity to come into our lives – those who live rich in gratitude for the spirit of life grow richer.

In the space below, write down what you value and what's important to you. When I did this exercise, I was able to see how important it is for me to feel like I make a difference to others through my speaking and writing talents. Therefore, I value *contribution*. Use what I call "green light thinking" and write down all that comes to mind. From there, list your values in order of priority and you will get a clear picture of what you value most in life and what ultimately drives you to attaining your dreams and goals.

Here's the question: *What makes your heart sing?*

The values you have listed bring light to all that you are. I hope you feel pride in what you have just done! Now put the items on your list in priority order with number one being the most important. Go with your initial feeling.

MONEY VALUES

The things we hold as valuable in our lives have impact on our relationship to money. As you consider the list you just made, ask yourself the following questions:

1) What does money provide that makes it such an important part of my life?
2) What does my answer from Question One provide that makes it such an important part of my life?
3) What does my answer from Question Two provide that makes it such an important part of my life?
4) What does my answer from Question Three provide that makes it such an important part of my life?

For example, perhaps you think money is important because it provides security. And what does security provide? Perhaps it provides peace of mind. But what's important about peace of mind? Maybe it allows you to be creative. Why do you want to be creative? Maybe creativity allows you to live your dreams.

As you work through this series of questions, you are placing your views or attitudes about money in a position where they hold true value for you. Not your parents, not your neighbors, just you. By creating a *values priority staircase*, you may begin to see how wildly out of sync your current patterns and behaviors are with your core values. From there, it's much easier to see what needs to change, and how positive change impacts your life for the better.

TRASH AND BASH – THE TRUTH ABOUT NEGATIVE THINKING

What you think about, you talk about.
What you talk about, you bring about.
– Anonymous

WHAT'S "ON" YOUR MIND?

You've either heard it or said it: *Thoughts are Things.* The words we speak or repeatedly think have power and energy. Our subconscious mind carries no judgment or discretion – it simply sets about creating a reality – our own reality – that corresponds to the commands we feed it.

Statistics show that more than 45,000 thoughts cross our minds each day, and that for the majority of people, the ratio of negative-to-positive thoughts is three to one. There is no such thing as an "idle" thought. "I'll never make enough money to afford a house in *this* neighborhood" will keep you forever in a dead-end job and sleeping in a second-floor walk-up. "I can't resist a sale" guarantees you'll always have an overstuffed closet and a deflated wallet. What you repeatedly tell yourself manifests.

We tend to lapse into negative self-talk during periods of stress or change, when something doesn't turn out as we had expected, or when our behavior is unproductive. Start paying close attention to what you tell yourself each day, and the potency of your negative thoughts. Get a golf game going in your head – your negative chatter represents the sand traps, water and roughs of the terrain – the longer you play the game, the more confident and experienced you become in selecting the most appropriate iron, the proper stance. The more you practice, your swing improves. When you find yourself thinking "Yes, I need to save for my son's college education, but he needs the best of everything right now" or "Yes, I want to save for retirement but my spouse spends money like water," catch yourself. See how differently you complete those thoughts when you replace "Yes, but…" with "Yes, *and*…" *And* requires you to take responsibility. *But* allows you to make excuses and place blame. Note how different you feel. I'll bet that using the word "Yes, *and*" fills you with a sense of power.

Nothing in this world is really black-and-white; replace *All or Nothing* thinking with *Something is Better than Nothing*. Think in terms of the choices you've made for yourself and how you can change those that no longer serve you. Remember, we are striving for *progress*, not perfection. The Chinese have an adage that says "Fall down once, stand up twice." When you find yourself thinking *I'm broke*, counter that thought with *I always have plenty of money*. Before you know it, you will not only say it, you'll believe it *and* have it! Why? Because you'll become more conscious and aware if your actions are congruent with what you truly desire. When you need a little help – try walking around the shopping mall with a $100 bill in your pocket. Count the number of things you can afford right now and *feel* the difference of knowing what it's like to always have choice.

THE BEST EXCUSE FOR STAYING STUCK

Everyone has doubts and limiting beliefs – you're not alone. The key is to keep them from taking over, to not let them keep us from moving forward. Limiting beliefs can keep us in debt or living paycheck-to-paycheck; they have the power to squash our precious dreams. Pretend you are a world-famous actor, on stage in the most important, dramatic role of your life. You're playing a long-suffering, pathetic creature who has been, and will forever be, stuck in a miserable existence. Read the following statements aloud in your very best nasal-filled whine.

- I'll never earn much money because I'm not a college graduate.
- My parents never taught me about money so I'm doomed to be in debt forever.
- I'm too old to start investing.
- If I had the kind of money *they* have, I could be investing like they do.
- My dream will never happen because I don't have enough money to fund it.

Sound familiar? Is a queen-size violin playing in the background? These are some of the most common limiting beliefs we can hold when it comes to money. I don't mean to trivialize anyone's excuses, I just want to illustrate how our limiting beliefs create the story that takes over and creates our realities. I can't emphasize enough that if your story doesn't serve you, it's time to get a new one!

Use the space below to record the negative money-talk and limiting beliefs that are racing through your brain. If you hear yourself thinking this exercise is pointless or it's not going to make any difference, I guarantee you'll feel very differently when you see the extent of your self-defeating thoughts staring back at you on paper.

What feelings and physical sensations came up while you wrote? It's important to remember how you felt so you won't want to return to that place. Albert Einstein said that problems cannot be solved at the same level of thinking in which they were created. We need to be aware of our limiting beliefs and the thinking that created them in order to move to a perspective in which we can deconstruct them and create new, positive ones.

Now take a break and some deep breaths. You're doing a great job!

BRIGHT AND LIGHT – THE POWER OF THE POSITIVE
When you've had enough of standing in the darkness, turn on the light. Let's talk about money in a new way. For every negative statement on your list, start listing a positive replacement, a statement you will use to fill up the space formerly held by the negative thought. Positive statements are called Affirmations or Statements of Being. Let me explain a little more about them.

An affirmation is a statement of *who you are*, and can be for you or against you – only you can make that choice. When we're not sure of who we are, we are vulnerable to what others have to say about us. Everyone has heard, either internally or externally, statements such as this: "You can't do that," or "How are you going to make any money doing THAT?" These statements are a mirror of self-doubt, and when you hear them or say them, it's important to look yourself or that other person in the eye and say, "Thank you for sharing and excuse me while I do." The Chinese have another adage: *Those who say it cannot be done should not interrupt those who are doing it*. Remember – what you think about you talk about, and what you talk about you bring about. Affirmations always begin with "I am," which is to acknowledge that we are sufficient and capable as who we are now. No positive change will occur until we believe that in our hearts. Oprah Winfrey says, "We are what we believe," and I fully agree. The choice then becomes a matter of what we *choose* to believe.

Write your thoughts in a calm, orderly fashion. List both positive and negative beliefs. Your mind will want you to edit, but continue writing freely. Download everything!

I believe the following to be true about myself:

_____

_____

_____

_____

Now that you know what you believe about yourself, it's time to reframe these beliefs into statements of being so that you can use them to make positive changes in your life.

Your next exercise is to create your own affirmations, also referred to throughout the book as "Diva Speak". Go back to the limiting beliefs you listed in the previous section. Take each one and reframe it into a positive. In addition, create a few new ones that support your values and dreams.

Here are a few sample affirmations we re-framed from some of the most common limiting beliefs:

Limiting Belief: I'll never earn much money because I'm not a college graduate.

Affirmation: I am capable of making all the money I need to fulfill my dreams.

Limiting Belief: My parents never taught me about money so I'm doomed to be in debt forever.

Affirmation: I am financially free and creating the money to live my dreams.

Take your sheet of affirmations to the printer and have it copied and laminated. Place your affirmations in strategic positions at home or at work where you will see them often. You may find it helpful to make wallet-sized copies to carry with you. Keep them visible and repeat them constantly and consistently. Post them in the shower, in the bedroom, or on the bathroom mirror where you are sure to see them every day. Remember – out of sight, out of mind – and those limiting beliefs are back. Every time you speak your affirmations, put a smile on your face, and a skip in your step. Feel them in every cell of your being, believe them with all your heart, and expect them to manifest!

DREAM COLLAGE
Collect the same types of materials you used for your First Step Collage, but forget about the credit card and bank statements – this one is meant to be much more fun. Create a relaxing environment – play a favorite CD while you're busy creating your dream. Clip pictures from magazines and catalogs that represent your dream. Insert a favorite photo of yourself, and include a few of your affirmations. Part of your dream can be a final destination, but make sure to include images of what your everyday life will be like now. As you're browsing, be mindful of what is important to you and what really makes you happy. Is it really having a new SUV? Is it having enough money stashed away that you can work part-time or volunteer, or having the latest and greatest toys? Is it being able to spend more time with your partner or children, or traveling the world? Let your mind wander.

The past has no hold on you now – unless you grant it power. Your future is limitless!

When you're done, sit back and take a good look – is your collage filled with bright images and words? Is it colorful and exciting? If you found this exercise more of a chore than a joy, revisit your money myths and biography. Can you pinpoint events or patterns that led to thoughts such as "I'll never have it, so why think about it?" We are so often filled with the belief that we can never achieve our dreams that we are afraid to give them life and form. We lock them in a dark, damp closet and when they do slip out, their arrival in our thoughts is greeted with despair rather than joy. Keep your dream collage handy – you'll be using it in the next exercise. Above all, the day by day journey is as important as the final destination, and every moment savored will make your arrival all the more gratifying.

100 THINGS THAT I WOULD LOVE FOR MY LIFE
This is one of my favorite exercises. It's very simple, and requires tapping into your heart and imagination a bit differently. List 100 things you would love to have or do or be in your lifetime. It's likely that part of your list will include things that require money, but others may not. Keep your Dream Collage in view while making your list, and let yourself have free rein – imagine you have just arrived on Fantasy Island – you *can* have *whatever* you want – nothing is too hard, to wild, too out-

rageous or too expensive. Do you want to climb the Eiffel Tower? Deliver a $500 donation to your favorite charity in person? Do you want the simple pleasure of a sunset picnic dinner with your family? Are you longing to become a marathon runner? Include a few things that you can realistically accomplish within the next year, but don't hesitate to list a vacation in the south of France, or sky-diving over the Great Barrier Reef, or anything else that has followed "someday, I'd like to…" in your mind or your words.

In every life, and in every generation, there are events that change the face and flavor of our dreams and beliefs. We've begun a closer examination of what is *really* important in our lives, and this exercise will most likely show you where your priorities have changed. The most crucial point is in holding to our ability and willingness to dream, against all apparent odds and in spite of the conditions around us. Dream big.

I like to keep this list posted so I can refer to it regularly. In fact, you may want to add a room to your home or create more wall space to post all of your affirmations and collages! It's time for green-light thinking again – imagine you're on the *Freedom Highway* and there are hundreds of miles of road ahead of you without a single stop light – all you have to do is step on the gas and go, as long as you want to, and at whatever speed makes you happy. If coming up with a list of 100 seems overwhelming, acknowledge that and keep going, one dream at a time.

FILL IN THE GAP

Put your two collages next to each other. They represent *where you are right now* and *where you want to be*. In between is the GAP. Reinventing your relationship to money means becoming so clear about where you've been and where you're going that the GAP is a welcome space, a time to savor all that you have to do – and be grateful that in each moment you are *already* enough.

I think of the GAP as an elastic band. If we don't fill it with action steps and tighten the band, we revert back to the familiar, comfortable habits that created our discomfort in the first place. Nature abhors a vacuum – we want to pull it tight and fill it with positive actions that move us toward our goals and dreams.

To show how this works, choose three items from your *100 Things* list. For each of the three items, you will complete one *Creating What Matters* sheet. Each sheet will contain the following information:
1) Vision or End Result with a due date
2) Current Reality
3) Action Steps with due dates
We're now asking, "*How* Can I?" instead of "Can I?"

Here is an example:
1) Vision or End Result with a due date: I would like to take a trip to California and need $3,000 by June 7.
2) Current Reality: I am $2000 in credit card debt and need to pay it off before I start saving for my trip.
3) Action Steps with due dates:
    a) Create debt-eliminating strategy and pay $400 every month toward my debt until the debt is paid off by November.
    b) Collect tourism brochures on California and read all I can by August.
    c) Decide what cities I'm most interested in visiting and learn about them by September.
    d) Determine the true cost of the trip by researching airfares, hotels and other expenses in books and on the Internet by October.
    e) Determine ways to cut some of the trip expenses by November.
    f) Put together savings plan by November.
    g) Save required amount by June.

Your action steps should be disciplined, but also fun. In this case, taking the time to learn about the cities keeps me excited about the process. Once you've completed the sheet for three of your *100 Things* items, stand up and stretch, then give a hearty round of applause to yourself for breaking the task down into simple, easily attainable steps. Then give yourself another round of applause because even though the steps you wrote may not be *perfect*, those sheets represent the very core of this program: progress.

FILL IN THE GAP

My Vision / End Result / Due Date: _____

My Current Reality: _____

WHERE I WANT TO BE: _____

ACTION STEP 4: _____
DUE DATE: _____

ACTION STEP 3: _____
DUE DATE: _____

ACTION STEP 2: _____
DUE DATE: _____

ACTION STEP 1: _____
DUE DATE: _____

WHERE I'M AT: _____

CHAPTER 4
HAVE A DREAM

*"Go confidently in the direction of your dreams!
Live the life you imagined."*

Thoreau

DIVA SPEAK:
I am capable of attaining my money goals with E.A.S.E.

Oblivio never paid attention to specifics and never really settled down to diagnose what he wanted, why he wanted it or how he could set about getting it. All he knew was that throughout his life he wanted more money – but couldn't quite explain his intent or demonstrate any ability to generate more funds. Then he met **Prospera**, a beautiful and energetic woman with a passion for skiing the mountains of British Columbia and a detailed method of making sure she was able to master the moguls at least once each winter. Oblivio learned that even though he resisted setting goals and being specific, money had to be *for* something. He believed Prospera when she told him knowing this and *not* doing anything about it was the same as not knowing it at all. Oblivio learned about goal setting, and got specific about his desire to accompany his new love on a ski trip he never thought he could afford. Within three months, Oblivio saved $500 for the trip; he and Prospera were last seen laughing together in a Whistler chair lift, and rumor has it that they're heading off to the Swiss Alps next winter.

Society defines success by material possessions and *perceivable* net worth – a definition that creates enormous pressure as we measure and judge ourselves in relation to what others have and what we don't have – or vice versa. We want to project an image of success, so we rent a lifestyle – we pay dearly for the upscale neighborhood zip code, the sporty car, the designer clothes, whether we can afford to sustain them, whether they "fit" our inner world or not. This is how we get caught up in a cycle of unwanted debt.

The real measure of success is *self worth*, and the belief in who you are – everything else is secondary. Instead of looking *at* the balance in our bank account, we are looking *through* the ancient Chinese coin. When your personal and inner foundation is strong and secure, the outer manifestations of success are at your disposal. We all aspire to different ways of life; it's fruitless to play a comparative game. Would you ever consider a tree more successful than a flower because it has more leaves? Success isn't *what happens to you*, but rather *what you make happen to you*! Reinventing your self worth will, in turn, prosper your net worth, creating a lifestyle that is abundantly successful.

In Chapter 3 we discussed the importance of having dreams that are in sync with our values. We're going to put those dreams in motion by creating a realistic money plan. Now it is time to put those dreams in motion. In this chapter, I'll teach you to set a vision for yourself, a vision that will align you with your desired state, help you create and maintain excitement about your plan, and move you from your present condition to your personal field of dreams – or ski slope, as the case may be. Remember, knowing without taking action is the same as not knowing at all.

DREAM WHEELS

A favorable mix of components on the Dream Wheel determines the outcome of your money plan.

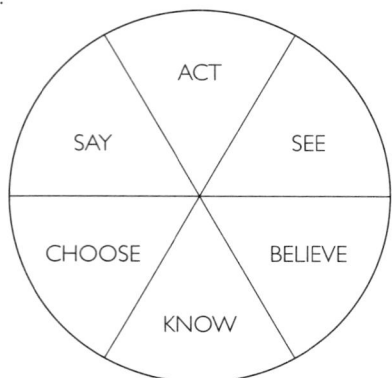

I like the analogy of a wheel because life is a continuous journey, and reinventing your relationship to money is a journey within the journey. Just like baking a cake, we need all of the ingredients for the recipe to work. Most of us don't *consciously* think of all the components in the diagram, but when they're synchronized we can and will create our desired state – living our dreams. Ask yourself the following questions to make sure you have a clear perspective of each component and can develop a clear course of action:

- **See:** How do I see the outcome of this situation?
- **Believe:** Does it resonate inside of me? Do I *really* believe it? Can I feel the excitement?
- **Know:** Do I know what resources I can draw upon to make it happen?
- **Choose:** Am I aware of the options available to me? Have I looked at them all?
- **Say:** What is my positive affirmation for this goal/dream? Remember to include the positive adjectives that evoke emotions and feeling!
- **Act:** What action steps will I need to take and, what action steps am I *willing* to take?

Here's an example: *Your desired state is to pay off a $5000 credit card debt.*

- **See:** Picture yourself receiving a credit card statement with a zero balance! The money you once sent to the credit card company is now available to invest in your dreams instead of high interest payments.
- **Believe:** Create a feeling and belief *inside* yourself that it is *already done!*
- **Know:** Analyze the current situation and determine what you need to know about paying off the credit card balance. Are you getting the lowest interest rate available? How can you free up additional cash?
- **Choose:** You can either pay off the debt and start investing for your dreams, or your debt can be a never-ending cash drain. Remember, *YOU choose!*
- **Say:** Repeat your affirmations each day: "I am *easily* paying off my debt and *joyfully* working toward my dreams." Note

the use of the adjectives easily and joyfully to evoke emotion and feeling. Repeat the statement using the words *slowly* and *resentfully*. How did you feel this time around?
- Act: Start freeing up cash, sending in *accelerated* payments and getting clear about *your* future!

You will make your dreams a reality when you synchronize the Dream Wheel components with your dreams. The Dream Wheel applies equally well to other areas of your life that may need balance: physical, spiritual, home, career and relationships.

ARE YOU FUNDING A FLAT TIRE?

One thing that can flatten your Dream Wheel faster than a pin in a balloon is *fear*. We fear those around us won't think highly of us, or we won't be accepted if we don't have the latest and greatest homes, cars, clothes – the list is endless. This fear puts us in serious doubt of ourselves, and in serious debt.

There is actually a form of fear that is good. I started to recognize the difference between the two when I read "Embracing Fear" by Thom Rutledge. He writes about the Bully/Ally components of fear and says that we need to determine if our fears are playing the role of bullies or allies in any given moment. If we're being unexpectedly attacked in a parking lot and need to defend ourselves it is perfectly normal and often helpful to experience fear. In this situation, it's acting as an ally. It can provide the adrenaline that converts to strength that may help us fight off an attacker. But most of us also experience fears that serve as bullies. The kind of fears that come from not appearing acceptable to others, not living up to a certain standard and feeling inadequate. This type of fear comes from the voice of the critic – or the Monkey Mind (which we'll discuss in a later chapter) – and is a typical aspect of any type of change. We're afraid to fail so we don't even try. We're afraid to do what we dream of doing because it doesn't fit in with whatever standards we consider valuable in our society. Take a deep breath and think about your fears. Are they helping or hindering?

Fear can also be disguised as procrastination – always a killer of dreams. We are afraid to fail, and we can be just as equally afraid to succeed, however irrational that may sound. Remaining stagnant provides a level of comfort that is hard to overcome – it derives from the cultural myth that we are *better safe than sorry*. No matter how familiar that level of comfort is, if it is not your *desired* state it will not propel you in the direction of your dreams.

Perhaps you've set a goal of creating an investment account by the end of the year. The voice of Monkey Mind may whisper in your ear: "You've tried that before! It didn't work! Why do you think you can do it now?" Enter fear. Enter procrastination. Enter doubt. The result: No investment account.

Fear is an unwelcome guest that sucks our creative energies. You've probably seen this acronym before:
False
Evidence
Appearing
Real
I prefer this one from Thom Rutledge:
Face
Explore
Accept
Respond

Facing our fears takes courage. When we *explore* our fears we can determine if they are serving as bullies or allies. *Accepting* them means not turning back. This is where we are today and we can't turn back. And when we *respond* we move forward with purpose.

When we can *Face Everything And Respond*, another FEAR acronym that I like to use, we can move forward – we can move on with courage.

How do you *dismantle* fear? Pay attention to the sensations in your body when you feel fearful. It comes out in a nervous stomach, shallow breathing, a desire to run. Different strokes for different folks. Pay attention to your body and try the following:

Step 1: Stop what you're doing.

Step 2: Take a few deep breaths. As you exhale, say "All is well." Listen to your breath as you inhale and exhale.

Step 3: Imagine you are a *dispassionate observer*. Step out of the situation and look at it as if it were happening to your best friend instead of you.

Step 4: Think about what advice you would give that friend in this situation. Listen for the guidance and write it down.

Step 5: Revisit your values and dreams.
Step 6: Proceed from this new place and get back on your *Dream Wheel*.

This process is designed to bring you to calmness, where you can gain a new perspective of the situation. Fear is a part of life, an energy that will arise time and again. When you are clear about your dreams and can tell the truth about your situation, you minimize the power of fear and stay in the driver's seat. Keeping this in mind – it's easier to work through the experience. The process may feel mechanical at first, but will soon become automatic, taking only seconds to process. Each time you work through these steps, you will become more comfortable with the process and learn to recognize and eliminate fear quickly. Remember, learning any new skill or behavior takes practice, patience and discipline.

YOUR FINANCIAL CHIROPRACTOR – ALIGNING GOALS WITH DREAMS

Goals are the framework, the structure that takes us to our dreams. When the vertebrae of our spine are skewed or twisted out of place, we need an adjustment because our spinal fluid- the energy source of our body – cannot flow freely through the impediments. The same is true of our goals and their relationship to our dreams. A goal that is out of alignment with our dreams presents a challenge akin to a slipped disc in the spine.

We're making a visit to the *financial chiropractor* in the next exercise, a visit that helps us make sense of our challenges and realign our goals with our dreams.

F.A.S.T. GOALS

It's time to put your dreams on paper. During this exercise, it's important to have an end result, but it's equally important to dream about the process. Look at the images from your collage and write down what they are telling you. I use the acronym F.A.S.T. *not* because this is a quick process, but because you will be enjoying your journey, and will feel like you are making progress from the beginning. Keep the F.A.S.T. process in mind while you're completing this exercise:

Feeling: When you're writing down goals, get into your heart as well as your mind. Write with feeling and emotion and your dreams will become a reality. Make sure this goal feels exciting and right for you. It is the energy and power behind your feeling that will ultimately turn the desired goal into your reality.

Action Steps: Include specific action steps that propel you to your goal.

Examples: I will pay myself first with $50 from every paycheck. I will avoid the mall unless I have specific items on a shopping list. I will read MONEY Magazine for at least fifteen minutes per day. I will reward myself with a pedicure for every month that I stay on track.

See: When you can see where you're going, you are compelled to take action. Look at your Dream Collage and add to it regularly so your dream is visible. Hold these images and pictures in your mind so they are easily accessible when you are in need of inspiration and don't have the collage right in front of you.

Timeline: Your dreams and goals must have benchmarks. A timeline will remind you that the journey is as important as the destination, and that *patience* is a critical part of the process. You may feel everything is moving too slow, taking too long. In those moments, pause to reflect and discover what you have learned along your journey. Every experience is there to bring you a lesson.

Review your list of "Top 100 Things" from Chapter 3 one more time. Choose three items that require money goals, with which you can create three different savings timelines. For instance, choose one item with a six-month savings timeline, one with a two-year timeline and one with a five-year time-line. Include big *and* small items from your list.

Example: One of your dreams is to own your own home. How much money do you need? Ideally, you would like to have 20% of the purchase price saved for a down payment. If the home costs $140,000 you need a down-payment of $28,000. If this amount seems steep and out of reach for you, don't worry. With low down payment programs available from lenders, most first-time homebuyers put down 10% or less. Let's say your goal is to come up with a 10% down payment or $14,000 in three years. Simple math tells us you'll need to save $389 every month. Make sure to keep your money in a safe, easily accessible money-market account. As you're saving, research the areas where you would like to buy and learn all you can about home ownership. These steps should also be included in your specific goals:

- I will save $389 every month for three years in a money market account.
- I will go on one house-hunting trip every two months for the next three years.
- I will read two books on home buying in the next year.

I can hear your *Monkey Mind* right now. "You've blown it so many times before, how's all this going to help?" Goals can be hard to set. When the "what if" scenarios pour in, it's Monkey Mind costumed as self-doubt and confusion. You are not the mistakes you've made in the past! If you knew better, you would have done better. Politely thank *Monkey Mind* for sharing, turn down the volume knob and continue creating your dream.

If you have difficulty with this exercise, take the emphasis off of what you want to *do*, and focus instead on what you want to *learn*, who you want to *meet* or who you want to *be*. This perspective places a new dimension on goal setting and makes it much more exciting! When I first started speaking in front of crowds, I got caught up in the "do's of my speech. I was so involved with the little details – who was going to be in the crowd, what I was going to wear or who was going to introduce me, that I lost sight of what my true purpose was. It was when I started focusing on what I wanted to give the audience, what I wanted to learn from this experience and who I wanted to be that I felt powerful beyond belief.

BE PROACTIVE

It's guaranteed that the moment we learn something new, life catches us off guard at 100 miles per hour. To be *proactive* means knowing that unexpected events happen in our lives, and to recognize these events when they occur. When an unexpected event hits, take some deep breaths, and know that this, too, is part of the journey. Our ability to *balance* the many facets of our lives is a major factor in the steps we take to manage the events of our lives, and continue moving forward. Inaction is the killer of all dreams. Making mistakes are a given on the journey of life. Expect them and learn from them. I titled this chapter "Dreams in Motion" for a reason. Keep the process moving and be a dreamer in the true sense of the word – in thought, word, and deed.

CHAPTER 5
BALANCING ACT

*"Every time I close the door on reality,
it comes in through the windows."*

Jennifer Unlimited

CHAPTER 5 • BALANCING ACT

DIVA SPEAK:
I have all the time and money I need to feel secure and live my dreams.

As a single mom, **Feartensia** was always concerned about saving money, so she worked every overtime hour her company made available. There wasn't much time for her son, for her family, and certainly there was not a minute to spare for herself, if she was to earn enough money to keep afloat. She was a human zombie, going through the motions of a busy life without actually *living* a life. When her brother-in-law died unexpectedly, Feartensia realized it had been more than six months since they were last together for a family dinner. Her son had not seen his cousins in over a year because her work schedule did not allow time for the drive to the other side of the state for a visit. She realized that she barely knew her own son and that being in touch with him and his needs was the most important thing in her life. The fear of not having enough had driven her to a life in which she really had *nothing at all* in terms of the things and people that *were* her life. Feartensia chose to make a change, to live in a balance between plans for tomorrow and the joys of today. She cut back on the overtime, refinanced her mortgage for a lower monthly payment, and took her son across the state for a long weekend with aunts, uncles and cousins. These days, Feartensia lounges in her bathtub with a good book on Wednesday evenings, soaking up abundance and balance in her life.

In this hectic 21st century world we live in, we hear a lot about the challenges of balancing our busy lives. A balanced life varies from person to person so it's impossible to describe what it looks like in general terms. In this chapter, I will give you my idea of what a balanced life should look like and provide some probing questions for you to ask yourself to find out what it should look like for you.

From my perspective, the seven "vessels" of a prosperous life, in alphabetical order, are:
- career
- family
- love
- money
- personal
- physical
- spirit

The symbol of the ancient Chinese coin allows us to *look through* money, which serves as a portal through which we can examine not only our relationship to it but most importantly, our relationship to ourselves which includes the vessels listed above. When you consider the seven vessels, know that we are always free to choose the role each of these areas plays in our lives. *Personal freedom* is so rich in sense of self. And it is not bound to anything that society dictates. If we're in a job we despise, we have the freedom to quit and look for work elsewhere. Although we can't choose our biological family, we are free to determine the role certain family members play in our own lives or we can choose others to become our "family." We can choose to leave a love relationship that is no longer healthy. When we consider ourselves *at choice* we have all the power.

How do you spend your time and your energy? Are you always in a hurry, or like Feartensia, so consumed with having enough that you have nothing at all of importance? If we're always in a hurry, stressed and out-of-control, what can we do to bring our life back into balance?

When we're *proactive* we're making a choice to be in control. When we're *reactive*, the situation has taken control. We've discussed our dreams, and now we'll discuss methods to incorporate those dreams into your life. When you give yourself time to reflect and just *breathe*, you bring more energy, and thus, more money, into your life.

LIFE BALANCE
I have no time to spend with my family and friends.
I just don't have any fun any more.
My kids are grown and I don't really know them.
I don't know what I want in life.

If thoughts like these meander into your consciousness, it's time to take a look at the level of balance in your life. What do you hold as the outward signs of a balanced life? Money affects so many areas of our lives – we need to keep them all balanced, because they are the spokes of our internal wheel. When several spokes are out of alignment, the tire goes flat or you find your life making a gut-wrenching "thump" every time you turn the corner. Our money life is a reflection of how we manage all the vessels we carry. Each component impacts the big picture.

Take some time to write in your journal about the balance in your life, and the image you hold of how a balanced life *should* look. You're on the right track if your dreams and values from Chapter 3 are included here.

STEPS TO TIME MANAGEMENT
How many times have you said: " I wish I had more time," or "Where does all the time go?" or "I would do it if I only had the time." *If only* serves no purpose in our lives other than to create regret. This book is not about typical time management skills or trying to reorganize your schedule, but it does include taking time for yourself and making yourself a priority every day. Take five minutes for your morning ritual and just sit still. *Five minutes.* It will change the way you approach everything. We typically wake up with an obnoxious alarm, fill up with bad news from the TV or radio, and blanket ourselves with fury in a traffic jam. By the time we've been out of bed for one hour we've set ourselves up for chaos and are triggered by the most innocuous and innocent statement or circumstance. Unfortunately, this scenario can set the tone as well as the results for your day ahead.

Turn off the noise around you. If you have to wake up five minutes earlier, do it! Sit quietly, take note of what you have to be grateful for, what you'd like your day to be like, and from there – plan your day. Figure out what you can do for yourself, and when. Visualize how you want your day to play out. Some days you may have an hour to walk in the park, other days you may just have five minutes to meditate, but fit *yourself* into your day, *every day*. You'll be amazed at how taking five minutes each morning for yourself puts *you* in control; you are no longer a victim of circumstance. You will, at some point, begin to look forward to your time of peace and solitude. I like to just sit in bed, still and silent. And I don't turn on the television or radio. I can easily picture what my day will look like when I have silence and can focus. Pick a theme word for the day like *confident* or *powerful* or *peaceful* – anything you would like to incorporate more of into your life. If you have children, get up five minutes earlier and spend this important time for yourself. Five minutes in the morning is it all it takes to set the stage for a day that *you* make happen.

Throughout the day, pay attention to your physical sensations. As you *feel* yourself getting tense or anxious, give yourself one minute – *one minute* – to breathe deeply and fully. Deep breathing is such a simple act, but it is an incredibly powerful way to relieve stress and tension. Imagine yourself inhaling *relaxation* and exhaling *tension*. As you do this, picture *all* that's causing you angst gradually fading away and a soft, warm light washing over this picture screen. If you breathe in and out slowly and gently five or six times, you'll feel better.

When you open up your credit card statement and feel your stomach tense up – Stop. Take five deep breaths. Then think about ways to put yourself in control of the situation instead of letting it control you. So much of finding a solution to our problems is acknowledging that we feel we've lost control. We will discuss debt-reducing strategies later on, so rest assured that you will have a plan in place to make you the master of your debt rather than its servant.

You are a MASTER when:	You are a SERVANT when:
you know there is always choice	you believe you have no choice
you know you are in control of yourself	you believe another holds control
you know your value	you believe you have no value

PERSPECTIVE QUESTIONS
Perspective is how we choose to see a situation while we're in the midst of it. We do not become the situation and it is *not* who we are. If we can see the situation for what it is, we know that it is only temporary. It puts us in a proactive rather than a reactive state – and we are masters instead of servants. Let's look at the difference:
Ask yourself:
1) What is the worst possible outcome of this situation?
   Keep reducing the outcome until it seems *ridiculous*. If it's not a threat to your survival or your life – and very little is – then it's not worth holding it as a threat.
2) Am I *willing* to accept this outcome?
   Remember, being willing allows us to find solutions to our challenges.
3) What are my alternatives?
   When we realize that we always have *options* and *choices* before us, we can move to a solution – sooner, rather than later.
4) What advice would I give to a friend in this situation?
   Be your own best friend – you're more likely to have *empathy, compassion and a clear perspective.*
5) Am I spending ten dollars worth of energy on a ten-cent problem?
   Time and energy are the two most precious commodities in our lives. Look for solutions instead of magnifying the problems, and as the saying goes – *don't sweat the small stuff and it's usually all small stuff!*
6) Will I remember this event five years from now? Or even one year from now?
   The answer to this question is usually NO! Learn from the discomfort of the past and there is no need to jog down memory lane. We are supposed to learn from our experiences in life and move on.

TESTS
Life is a series of T.E.S.T.S.
We will be tested many times in life. During the writing of this book, I suddenly came down with bells palsy, and the left side of my face became

literally paralyzed overnight. Along with quite a bit of pain, I looked in the mirror and one side of my face was literally drooping. Half of my face smiled, the other had next to no movement. I felt so self conscious and started to play the *what-if* game. *What if* I had to speak in front of a group of people? *What if* I had to make a television appearance?

The doctor told me that it was all stress related. I certainly couldn't argue with that! I was so busy – trying to do too much and basically burning the candle at both ends. I needed to slow down and my body was telling me so.

All I could do that afternoon was sit in the sun and rest. As I was relaxing and trying to recover, I knew I was being tested. I was feeling pretty sorry for myself until all of a sudden something came to me, that I hope you will remember the next time you are tested:

In seeing this setback as a T.E.S.T.

I realized that it was **T**emporary.

I realized that I was going to use it to **E**mpower myself through all that I've been learning.

I knew that I needed to **S**urrender. I didn't have to do this on my own and the best thing I could do at this moment was absolutely *nothing*.

I needed to **T**rust. I needed full faith that I may not know what to do, but the universe knows. Oprah Winfrey said, "The universe will always dream a bigger dream for us than we can dream for ourselves." Doesn't that take a big weight off of your shoulders? I needed full faith that that I may not know what to do in this moment, but the universe knows.

Finally, I needed to allow the love and **S**upport of those around me to overcome and take the next step.

THREE REALITIES

- Live for today – forget about tomorrow.
- Live for tomorrow – forget about today.
- Live for today – plan for tomorrow.

Each of us has chosen to live one of these realities. Which one are you living now? Write it down. Which one do you want to live? Why? Write it down. For me, staying in the present has been one of the biggest challenges. In times of stress, it can be easy to shut down and avoid the *pain of the past* or the *fear of the future*. It is in these times that I especially need to remember how important balance is and to know with certainty that I am *not* my past mistakes and that I *am* in control of my future.

Create your future by letting go of the negative experiences of your past and to consciously create in each present moment. As long as you are clear on what you want to create and why, you don't have to know how. It will miraculously come together.

One thing I know to be true is that *fear* appears when we dwell on our past, or make assumptions about the future – *fear* cannot reside in the present moment. Knowing this, life becomes a conscious decision to learn from the past but dwell in the present. It is our awareness, intention and actions that ultimately shape our future, bring about balance and provide the foundation for our self-worth *and* our net-worth.

CHAPTER 6
WORTHY AND WONDERFUL

"We don't see who we are until we can see what we can do."

Martha Grimes

DIVA SPEAK:
I am abundant in my self worth and my net worth.

Most of the time, **Lackwanno** felt poor. His friends bought fashionable new clothes, drove new cars, and traveled. By comparison, Lackwanno felt inferior as a man and in his ability to earn enough money to enjoy the same life as his friends. Waiting for the bus on a particularly depressing day, Lackwanno noticed a little boy who looked much like himself as a child. He laughed out loud as the boy chased an autumn leaf down the street. Struck by the simplicity of his delight, Lackwanno began to make note of the things that made him feel good. That evening, he listed everything he enjoyed during the day – the neighborhood cat who welcomed him home with a purr, the smell of fresh-cut grass, the warmth of clean socks fresh from the dryer. The next day he noticed he was grateful for his walk to the bus stop. While his friends paid fees to work out on health club machines, he was getting exercise and enjoying the fresh air, for free. Within days Lackwanno was listing three, five, sometimes even ten reasons for gratitude each day, writing them joyfully in a journal. His world changed; within months he had a new job with a company that offered training, and was on the way to making more changes in his financial picture.

HOW MUCH ARE YOU WORTH?

A common myth in our culture is that when we have a certain measure of *net worth*, we automatically have an equal measure of *self worth*.

While I agree that there is a significant connection between the two, I take exception to the order in which they manifest. In my world, a strong sense of *self worth* contributes to a strong measure of *net worth*.

In addition to creating and funding our "financial" bank accounts, we also need to create and fund our "emotional" bank accounts. Instead of simply looking *at* a flat coin, we're looking *through* the window of the ancient Chinese coin.

It's easy to be hard on ourselves. It's also easy to put everyone else first in our lives, since that is what we're taught. Since you may not be doing anything significant for yourself at this moment, I'm going to start small. I'm going to ask you to spend a mandatory five minutes out of your day, every day to sit still and be with yourself. Take this five-minute period and picture how your day is going to go. This is mandatory time for me every day. It's amazing what five minutes can do as you peacefully put yourself in a positive frame of mind. I like to think of my five minutes in the morning as deposits into my emotional bank account. Here are some other things to try:

- Speak Diva Speak! Be nice to yourself and say nice things about yourself – quietly in your own head and aloud to others. Even if you don't feel very good about yourself at the moment, speak nicely anyway. How you treat yourself will directly impact how you treat others.
- Feel the warmth of a job well done. After completing something, take a moment to feel great about what you've accomplished. Step back and pause to inhale what you've created.
- Build an "emotional treasure chest" that you can dip into when necessary. When I find myself getting frustrated or angry about something that is completely out of my control, I have a few things I tap into to bring myself back to reality. I think about my loving mother and I picture myself holding her hand. It calms my nerves and puts whatever "moment" I'm having on hold. This one takes practice – it's hard to mentally bring yourself out of a stressful moment like this, but the more we do it the more natural it becomes. Choose a few nice memories or thoughts and practice getting them into your head when you need them the most.

There are two ways of living our lives – with a *BIG* S or a *little* s. When we live in the realm of "self" with the little s we are simply reacting. When we are "SELF" with a capital S, we are responding. When we respond, we are in control. When we react, we typically give away control and our power to others. Our personal freedom comes from being willing to put ourselves first and to always know that we are at choice.

SELF vs. self

SELF WORTH = HOW WE FEEL ABOUT OURSELVES, REGARDLESS OF FINANCIAL STATUS.

"Financial well being is not measured by how much we have, but by how we *feel* about how much we have." When I saw this quote on a bank brochure, I wanted to stop in and thank them. We live in a competitive culture, a world that changes quickly – it is easy and common to think of ourselves in terms of our income. We identify with our peers and feel we need to "keep up" with our neighbors, not stopping to realize that they quite possibly are trying to keep up with us! That's the Catch-22 of perceived value – the insidious cycle of stress and striving – we're caught in it and most often, too numb to see the impact it has on our lives.

True self worth comes when we cut through blame and shame, and know that we always have the resources within us to feel good about ourselves. Look at the life of Rosa Parks. As a young black woman in the segregated south, she refused to give up her bus seat to a white man. Her simple, individually-driven act stands, these decades later, as the starting point of a movement that changed the face of America once and for all. I sincerely doubt that Ms. Parks sat on that bus thinking her act of defiance would have impact on anything but her own weary body. But one thing I know for sure is that Ms. Rosa Parks, although never a significantly wealthy woman, had a greater sense of self worth than many a millionaire.

When our inner Self matches the one we show to the world, we are able to manifest our dreams. All of our relationships improve because we are not trying to put on a show or deceive others. And that's when we make the good choices that are right for each of us.

SELF WORTH EXERCISE

The qualities you admire in others are a good indication of who *you* really are – that is why you are attracted to those people. Take some time now to make a list of the people you admire, and the qualities they possess.

One of the people on my list is Oprah Winfrey, a woman who has used the traumas and hardships of her early life as springboards to her current standing as one of the wealthiest women in the world – financially, emotionally and spiritually. Dynamic, committed to improving other's lives, powerful, influential, and carrying a great sense of humor, Oprah Winfrey embodies the outcomes of awareness and practice set forth in this book, applied to every aspect of her life. She continues to be a great inspiration and role model for me and a multitude of others.

When your list is complete, examine it closely for patterns. Perhaps several people on your list are admirable because they are *honest*, or because they are *courageous*. Maybe the majority of them are *happy*. Whatever patterns you see in your list of admirable qualities in other people are the qualities *you* possess, whether you've brought them to the forefront of your life or not. Think about how you can incorporate more of these important qualities into your own life.

NET WORTH = WHAT WE OWN LESS WHAT WE OWE

Net worth is a relative number, showing your assets minus your liabilities – what you *own* less what you *owe* – at a specific moment in time. To determine our net worth, we place a value on all of our assets: home, car, savings, saleable works of art, furniture and other material possessions. Keep in mind that the *value* of our assets is the amount we could expect to receive if we sold them today, not the price we paid for them. You may have paid $3,000 for a living room set two years ago but its resale value today is only $300. Once we have determined the value of our assets, we add up our debts – mortgage, credit card balances, student loans, car loans, etc. When we subtract our total debt from our total assets, the result is our *net worth*.

Here's a simple example of positive net worth:

OWN	OWE
Home – $150,000	Mortgage – $125,000
Car – $6000	Car loan – $4000
Savings – $8300	Credit Card Debt – $0
Furniture – $2000	Student Loan – $6700
Computer – $1000	
Miscellaneous Items – $2000	
Total Assets: $169,300	**Total Liabilities: $135,700**

TOTAL NET WORTH: $169,300-$135,700 = $33,600

Here's a simple example of negative net worth:

OWN	OWE
Car – $6000	Car loan – $6000
Savings – $0	Credit Card Debt – $7000
Furniture – $1500	Student Loan – $5000
Miscellaneous Items – $1500	
Jewelry – $1200	
Total Assets: $10,200	**Total Liabilities: $18,000**

TOTAL NET WORTH: $10,200-$18,000 = (-$7,800)

Using these examples as a starting point, determine your net worth. Remember that this number is only a snapshot of where you stand financially *right now*. So many people let this number determine their position on the self worth scale – by now, you should be solid in acknowledging your *choice* in which direction your net worth, and equally important, your self worth, will move.

NET WORTH CHART

How much difference is there between what you own and what you owe? Use this chart to calculate your net worth now, and continue to use it in conjunction with the Net Worth Chart to map your progress and growth.

1) Insert the value of your assets, including home, car, savings, works of art, furniture, other possessions:

Description	Amount
	$
	$
	$
	$
	$
	$
	$
	$
	$
Total #1	$

2) Insert debts here: mortgage, car loans, student loans, credit card balances, other:

Description	Amount
	$
	$
	$
	$
	$
	$
	$
	$
	$
	$
Total #2	$
Subtract Total 2 from Total 1 for your Net Worth	$

NET WORTH PROGRESS CHART

Take a snapshot of your net worth every month, and post it on a chart – being able to see your progress is powerful incentive to keep going, and helps you maintain the hands-on approach to reinventing your relationship to money. Post your chart where you can see it often, celebrate your progress and remember that every dollar you spend in paying off debt is actually increasing your net worth!

NET WORTH

INSTRUCTIONS:

- Enter the current month in the first shaded box at the bottom, and continue with the rest of the months across the page.
- Enter the amount of your current NET WORTH in the bottom of the blank column at the left.
- As you calculate your net worth each month, enter the new amount in the boxes above your starting amount, and draw lines to graph out the changes as your Net Worth rises over the next year!
- Post this chart somewhere where you can access it easily and see it frequently.

THE RELATIONSHIP BETWEEN SELF WORTH AND NET WORTH

Although you may want to believe that your net worth determines your self worth, the opposite is true. Having a healthy sense of yourself is the first step to achieving your goals for *your* net worth. Fortunately, we can work on both simultaneously. We've all heard the stories of ordinary people who become multi-millionaires with the purchase of a single lottery ticket, and wind up flat broke a few years down the road. Their net worth, their instant riches, simply disappeared because they didn't change their habits or their beliefs about themselves. The same holds true for many people who've experienced bankruptcy. The likelihood of a second bankruptcy is greater because their money habits and their sense of self worth remained unchanged. We all need to learn, and believe, that we are valuable people regardless of the dollars in our bank account. Remember that money is here to serve us in living out our dreams.

Just like money, a positive sense of self doesn't grow on a tree. But like the delicate, perfectly round and graceful leaves of a money tree, a positive sense of self unfolds one turn at a time, supported by well-planted roots and fed daily doses of sunlight and water. Today, you are a seedling of a graceful money tree, and the work we are about to undertake are the steps that, one at a time, foster the gentle unfolding of your positive self.

First, that little, critical voice that nags at you with every positive thought you invoke – that voice that says "I'm never going to make enough money, I won't be good enough until I have a 6-figure bank account," and other debilitating statements. This little voice, called *Monkey Mind* in the Buddhist tradition, is powerful – and destructive. Let's get clear right now, before we dive into the next exercise. *Monkey Mind* has the maturity level of a 9 year-old child and seeks only two things – to *survive* and to *be right* – at all times, and at any expense. What helped me to calm the voice of the critic was to acknowledge that it will always be with me in some form or another, and that I have the power to twist the volume knob down, and that this voice has no more power in my life than that which I grant to it. When you learn to unplug your emotions from *Monkey Mind*, you recognize it's whining voice sooner rather than later, and have the ability to say *"Thanks, but no thanks."* So honor the times that *Monkey Mind* has served you well in the past, and honor the truth that you no longer need that type of advice. *Acknowledge* it rather than condemning it – that is, honor it to the point where it is content to be quiet.

When fear and *Monkey Mind* creep into my thinking, I remember Marianne Williamson's words in her book *A Return to Love:*
Our deepest fear is not that we are inadequate.
Our deepest fear is that we are powerful beyond measure.
It is our light, not our darkness that most frightens us.
We ask ourselves, who am I to be brilliant, gorgeous, talented and fabulous?
Actually, who are you not to be?
You are a child of God. Your playing small doesn't serve the world.
There's nothing enlightened about shrinking so that other people won't feel insecure around you.
We were born to manifest the glory of God that is within us.
It's not just in some of us: it's in everyone.
And as we let our light shine, we unconsciously give other people permission to do the same.
As we are liberated from our own fear, our presence automatically liberates others.[1]

So we are going to change the voice of the critic into the voice of a friend, one that will insulate us from the hissing, derogatory words of *Monkey Mind* and guide our thoughts and words to the positive – to constructive encouragement, honor and respect.

POOR VS. BROKE

Poor is a state of mind which can be permanent and fatal. *Broke* is a state of financial reality which is often temporary. They are not interchangeable terms.

Poor has to do with self worth, stemming from our belief system.

Broke has to do with net worth, providing an opportunity for us to learn and grow.

If you stay *poor* in your beliefs, you'll always stay *broke*.

1 Williamson, Marianne. A Return to Love, Harper-Collins Publishers, 1992.

Poor me and *J.O.B. — Just over broke* are two phrases that incorporate those words and attitudes. Say them both aloud and note how your feelings change. Also, pay attention to how those around you use these and other related phrases.

COST OF COMPARISON

Comparison works well in determining things like which automobile has the highest fuel efficiency rating, or whether you take the highway or the scenic route on your trip to grandma's house. When it comes to our self worth, comparison is a demon we are best to quickly exorcise.

You've no doubt heard the adage "he puts his pants on one leg at a time, just like any other man." The reality is we all eat, drink and sleep in basically the same way. We're similar at the core level — but the *cost of comparison* beyond whether you sleep on your side while your partner sleeps on his back can be steep. When you compare yourself to others, the scales always tip to the negative and hold us there, owning us, and the damage it leaves in its wake is the dissolution of self worth.

Contempt for ourselves is bred, like germs in a laboratory dish, on the negative emotions of *envy, fear, shame and victimization*. We need strong medicine to counteract the disease of contempt, and that medicine comes quietly and simply through *gratitude* and the heartfelt *knowing* that in every moment we have everything we *need* even though it may not represent everything we *want*. There will always be those with more, and there will always be those with less. Gratitude for the small and simple blessings in our lives allows us to create more and ultimately help others to do the same.

TELLING THE TRUTH

Another tool in the trade of conscious living is *telling the truth*, simply stating the facts as they are — no embellishment, no avoidance, and no honor whatsoever to the judging voice of *Monkey Mind*, which springs up with critical glee to say "You're not making enough money, and you're not *enough* to make enough money to pay off this debt" when you say "I owe $10,000 in credit card debt." We would never speak to a respected friend in the tone or manner in which we speak to ourselves. Stating the truth without a dramatic story line or excuses allows us to move on to positive action steps. An example of truth with clarity is, "I'm $10,000 in credit card debt, and it's important to me to pay it off."

Whenever we *don't* tell the truth we block creative energy and allow the critical voice to become louder. Telling the truth doesn't mean that you unload *unnecessary* information onto others. It doesn't even have to involve communication with other people – it primarily needs to resonate within *you*. The practice of telling yourself the truth builds integrity and promotes the ability to allow your intuition – the gentle voice within that knows the difference between truth and lie – to guide you. This is the voice that tells us to turn right instead of left, or to reschedule a meeting. This is the voice we need to rely on, to listen to intently; this is the voice of our creative partner in birthing a life of abundance and prosperity.

KEYS TO A STRONG SELF WORTH

According to Don Miguel Ruiz, author of *The Four Agreements*, there are four precepts involved in a strong self worth and living our dreams. He says we are all artists creating the landscapes of our lives. Review the agreements, then answer the questions that follow:

1) Be impeccable with your word. Speak in a truthful, non-critical manner and skip the gossip.

   Are you always impeccable with your word?

   When are you not?

2) Always do your very best. Be confident in knowing that any situation can change, because you believe it can change.

   Do you do your best in every situation?

   What areas could stand improvement?

3) Don't take anything personally. You may have $10,000 in credit card debt, but it doesn't become who you are.

   What situations do I take personally?

   How does it serve me?

How does it make me feel?

4) Never make assumptions. Don't assume that because you have $10,000 in credit card debt your options are limited and you will never be able to take a trip, shop for new clothes or build a future for yourself.

Why do I make assumptions?

How does making assumptions serve me?

In reality, our needs are few yet our wants are many. Life is about *simple living*. I have found that the more complex I make my life, the more likely I am to face greater challenges. As my life becomes simpler, I feel better about myself and experience more joy. What I have to offer from within is a gift I respect and cherish, and my sense of self worth is in that knowing.

A major part of the teaching in this book involves stripping away the layers of beliefs, attitudes and habits that keep us from experiencing the reality of who we are. You've come a long way already – we're about to pass the halfway mark in our journey, and one thing I know is that by this point, you've begun to get a grasp on what is really *real* for you. Congratulations!

CHAPTER 7
PROGRESS, NOT PERFECTION

*"We can do anything we want to do
if we stick with it long enough."*

Helen Keller

CHAPTER 7 • PROGRESS, NOT PERFECTION

DIVA SPEAK:
I am willing to track my expenses and record my progress with ease for the next 90 days.

Feartensia lived and breathed *a day late and a dollar short*. She worried incessantly, believing there was never enough money to go around. Her generous income and relatively low level of debt stood at odds with the fact that she was always short on money. Reluctantly, she agreed to track her spending and was absolutely amazed to see how much she frittered away on "stuff" – a magazine here, a pedicure there, clothes she never wore, lunches and dinners out on the town. After 90 days, Feartensia knew exactly where her money was going, and had become far more conscious of her spending. Today, she has a money surplus, and still enjoys her life because she's learned the value of discretionary spending. She knows where her money is, and knows how to spend it wisely.

Albert Einstein defined insanity as doing the same thing over and over again and expecting different results. In order to understand where the break in your money chain occurs, you have to have a clear image of every link. Tracking your expenses for 90 days and documenting your thoughts, habits and progress each day gives you rich data to analyze and ultimately act on.

Imagine taking a cross-country road trip without a map, in a car that had no gas gauge or speedometer. How would you know the distance you can cover in a single day? How would you know if you can make it to the next town without running out of gas? How would you know what freeway interchange takes you south of Chicago instead of straight downtown?

Learning about your current habits and patterns gives helpful insight in reinventing your relationship to money. The truth is that you can't develop an action plan until you have data to analyze, and the results of your analysis determine the details of your action plan. In our road trip model, you would document how many miles you drove today, how much gas you used and the routes you took. That information lays the foundation for your ability to gauge how far you can go tomorrow, and the most appropriate roads to keep you going toward your ultimate destination. Remember, knowing without awareness and an action plan is the same as now knowing at all!

MONEY TRACKER: YOUR 31-DAY FINANCIAL WALKABOUT
Aboriginal people across the globe follow varying forms of a common tradition. At some time in every person's life, they are required to experience a "coming-of-age" ritual in which they walk away from the tribe into the unknown, into the jungle, into the desert, into themselves, in order to learn their true calling or gain greater understanding of their world on their own. The Australian aborigines call this a "walkabout" – a journey of introspection, reflection, and mindful intent. In your Financial Walkabout, things will be a bit different – I won't ask you to fly to the South Pacific for a trek across the Australian continent, or wander aimlessly through the nearest forest. I *will* ask you to keep careful records of every penny you spend and the emotional states associated with your spending. Hold your agenda for a positive relationship to money very firmly in your head and heart, knowing that each penny you track, each feeling you document, is a step toward awareness of your spending habits and the role they have played in your life. When you return from your Walkabout 31 days from now, your financial world will be changed, because your perception and understanding changed.

The "miscellaneous" column in most people's budgets is usually the largest, because we don't have a clue where the greatest part of our dollars actually goes. You know you withdrew $100 from the bank three days ago. You know that today, seventy-two hours later, a lone five-dollar bill sits in your wallet. For the life of you, you can't remember where you parted company with the other ninety-five bucks, so you log it under "miscellaneous," if you log it at all.

When we are aware of what we have available to us and the patterns in which we spend, we can make better decisions, gain control and self-confidence, and ultimately be happier.

A Financial Walkabout helps you see if you are spending your money mindfully on things that are important to you, or mind-less-ly on things that are not. I know you're probably thinking "This is too boring! I'm going to quit! Why should I track every cup of coffee or *People Magazine* I purchase?" I know that walking across your financial continent is a tedious, time-consuming process, but just like any other form of exercise, the movements you learn soon become habit, and over time, the effects are dramatic. Think of it as the greatest adventure of your financial life, and take it one day, one week, one month at a time. You'll be amazed to find that daily $3 cup of coffee is actually $90 per *month*, or that lunch with friends twice a week adds up to $2,000 each year.

This exercise is not meant to tell you how to spend your money or force you to stop spending altogether. If that $3 cup of coffee is important to you, by all means have it, but *be aware* of the expense and the ultimate value it carries in your life.

I've supplied 31 days worth of cash trackers in this chapter to get you started. The forms contain sample categories – there may be items that don't apply to your life and those you will need to add. Try and create categories that really represent a typical month. Are you ready? Here are three simple rules to follow:

- During your Walkabout, avoid credit card purchases. Use cash, checks or a debit card. If you absolutely *must* use a credit card, immediately write a check for the amount you charged, and deduct if from your bank account balance.
- Each night, drop one dollar in a jar if you have successfully tracked your expenses. At the end of your Walkabout, you will, hopefully, have $31 to gift yourself with something wonderful.
- Maintain the Walkabout Journal outlined below. It's just as important to track our emotions as it is to track your actual expenses.

READY – SET – HAVE FUN!!!

Debt Free Diva Cash Tracker for:															
	1	2	3	4	5	6	7	8	9	10	11	12	13	14	15
FOOD															
Groceries															
Breakfast															
Lunch															
Dinner															
Snacks															
Coffee															
Drinks after work															
ENTERTAINMENT															
Movie rentals															
Movies															
Concerts															
CDs															
Books															
Magazines															
Sports events															
Casino															
Flowers															
Electronics															
Gifts															
TRANSPORTATION															
Gas															
Car Wash															
Parking Fees															
CLOTHING															
Work items															
Play items															
Shoes															
Special Events															
Dry cleaning															
PERSONAL CARE															
Manicure															
Pedicure															
Hair															
Make-up															
Gym membership															
OTHER															

16	17	18	19	20	21	22	23	24	25	26	27	28	29	30	31	Total

THE WALKABOUT JOURNAL

Your journal coincides with your money tracker, with an entry for each of the next thirty-one days. The progress journal puts your thoughts on paper so you can see the changes in your thinking that correspond to the changes in your spending. Remember we are after *progress* not *perfection*, and your journal is for your eyes only. Tell the truth. I'm asking you to create and incorporate a ritual into your life for at least 31 days. Continue with it beyond that point, if you find it useful. Copy the form freely!

I keep my journal at my bedside, completing my entries before I rise in the morning. You may choose to make yours an evening ritual – use whatever method makes it easiest for you to follow through each day. Your mind is probably telling you, "How can I find time to write every day with my busy schedule?" I suggest to you that you don't have the time *not* to do this exercise, and remind you that you are not being asked to write the Great American Novel. On days you waiver in completing your journal entry, review your personal contract and remember that you agreed *to be willing*. It takes approximately 21 days to create a new habit and I guarantee you your daily journaling will become a welcome part of your day!

The five items below give you a good start on what to document in your journal. They assume an evening ritual, and are easily transposed if you choose to work in the morning:

1) Review your *affirmations* list. Speak them aloud three times and write them in your journal.
2) Spend a few minutes reflecting on your day. Take as much time as you need to let your pen flow and get your feelings on paper.
3) List at least three things you were grateful for during this day. This exercise puts us in a position of being thankful for what we have, regardless of our financial situation. Some days it's easier than others – in fact, some days I'm just grateful the day is over!
4) List at least three things that you can do tomorrow that will make you feel great.
5) Write down one positive behavior change you made that day – no matter how small you think it is.

CHAPTER 7 • PROGRESS, NOT PERFECTION

One of the benefits of a Walkabout is that regardless of how far we go, or how close we stay to home, we are *moving*, and movement is the activator of our dreams.

CHAPTER 8
GET REAL

*"Money isn't everything…
but it ranks right up there with oxygen."*

Rita Davenport

DIVA SPEAK:
I handle my money with E.A.S.E. and always have money available.

Spenderella left the office feeling particularly bad about a negative comment from a co-worker. She went straight to the mall then headed home laden with bags and two credit cards that threatened to explode from overuse. As she unpacked her purchases, she experienced something odd. Shopping had always made her feel good, but this time it didn't. With each sweater and skirt she pulled from the bags, she found herself thinking "I don't really need this," and "I could use the money I paid for these shoes as an extra deposit in my money market account." Spenderella felt a rush through her body when she came to the thought "What if I just *returned* all this stuff?" The next day she did just that, and realized the methods she used in the past to appease her feelings of worthlessness and disappointment were no longer appropriate. She had taken control of herself in a new way, and taken steps to living her dreams sooner rather than later. The co-worker, by the way, apologized.

AS YOU PERCEIVE, SO YOU BELIEVE

The mere thought of tracking expenses makes most people roll their eyes with dread, so they never really get a good look at the difference between what they *think* they are spending – perceived expenses – and what they are *actually* spending. With the help of the documentation from your Financial Walkabout – your cash tracker sheets, we're going to find ways to free up additional cash every month, based on your individual circumstance. Before we get started, go back to Chapter Two and review the information on E.A.S.E. Have you begun to utilize this formula in your life and relationship with money? Which areas are working best? Which needs more of your attention? Remember E.A.S.E. stands for **E**ducation, **A**ction, **S**upport and **E**nergize.

FREEING UP CASH

Take a serious look at your expenses in your Daily Cash Tracker and do the following:
- Highlight anything that appears excessive or wasteful. One of the things I found I could do without was a weekly magazine I rarely read.
- Highlight anything that isn't a necessity or doesn't match up with your dreams and values. Again, for me it was the magazine, a small weekly amount, but totaling over $200 for the year.
- Remember to tell the truth. Make sure to include *everything* – even a fifty-cent newspaper. It may seem trivial to you on its own, but you may be "nickel and diming" yourself out of your dreams.
- Remember that trimming expenses is about moderation, not deprivation. You always have choices and what it comes down to is how *in love* you are with your dreams. After making only minor, conscious lifestyle changes, you'll be *amazed* at how much cash you will free up. But it takes being conscious and aware.

A friend of mine reported changing three things immediately:
- She had been purchasing a $3 cup of cappuccino six times per week – totaling $18. That may not sound like much, but she chose to cut back to two days a week and freed up **$624 for the year**. ($3 x 4 days x 52 weeks = $624.) And something unexpected happened – she began to enjoy the cappuccino even more because it became a treat instead of the routine.
- She had maintained, but rarely used, a $50 per month gym membership. She began walking and jogging every day instead, cancelled the membership and freed up **$600 in a year**. ($50 x 12 months = $600)

- She then decided to analyze her phone bill, and found $15 in extra services she never used. She freed **$180 each year** without missing a beat. ($15 x 12 months = $180)

Imagine – by analysis of her cash tracker, telling the truth about how important these items were in her life, and three relatively small changes in spending, she saved $1,404.

Investing $1404 each year for 15 years with a 8% rate of return = $38,122. *Now that's real dream money.*

(Note that 8% is used for example only. There are no guarantees that this rate of return is attainable.)

Everyone is different and will find different expenses to modify or eliminate. Your $3 cafe latte may be a social expense that you're *not* willing to give up. That's OK. But would you be willing to meet yourself halfway – have *fewer* lattes – and be able to meet your dreams? The point is to be *aware* of where your money is going. Your spending should coincide with your real necessities and your real dreams. Here are a few common expenditures that you may want to consider reassessing when looking for areas to free up cash:

- Magazine off the newsstands versus subscriptions, versus shared subscriptions
- Cable television – are you watching *all* the channels you're paying for?
- Dinners out versus cooking in. Just for fun, calculate how much you spend eating out.
- Lunches out versus brown-bagging it
- New books versus used books versus library books
- Movies out versus video rentals
- Clothes you buy on impulse
- A *fifth* pair of black dress shoes!

Here are some other cash-freeing stories I've heard:
- Joanna started sharing books and magazine subscriptions with a friend.
- John chose to bring his lunch two days a week instead of going out every day. He made his *brown-bag* days special by meeting a friend in the park for lunch.

- Debbie was making too many impulsive shopping choices and decided to leave the tags on any new clothes she purchased for at least a week. The week gave her time to determine if the clothes were really important to her.

One note about gift giving. With the pressure to keep up with our neighbors, we can get a distorted perception of gift giving and may find it necessary to go overboard when purchasing gifts. It may feel great in the moment, but we need to consider how we'll make the payments. A great way to free up cash is to consider some creative ways to give that really come from the heart. How about offering a day of house cleaning to a busy mother? What about offering a full day to spend with your kids without interruptions? There are many ways to free up cash and be creative and generous at the same time! Gift-giving is a reality. Consider establishing a "gift account" to which you contribute a specified amount each month. Determine how much you are willing to spend on gifts for the year, and divide that amount by twelve to compute your monthly deposit. Include this amount in your spending plan. Pre-planning your gift giving reduces the stress you feel when faced with another expenditure!

Create your own *What if* scenarios. What if I gave up those magazine subscriptions? What if I cut back on lunches out? What if I cancelled my cable television? Are there automatic expenses in your life that you could reconsider? List the expenses *you* could eliminate from your Daily Cash Tracker here:

How much cash can you free up by elimination or reduction of minor expenses? How much quicker could you pay off your debt and/or invest in your dreams if you made a few simple changes in the way you spend? I guarantee you will feel better about yourself as you see your debt decrease dollar by dollar – and watch your net worth increase at the same rate.

What if I...	Current Amount	New Amount	Savings Per Month	x 12 = Per Year
bought café latte once a week instead of five days a week?	$15.00 per week	$3.00 per week	$48.00	$576.00

SPENDING PLAN

Forget about *budgeting*, at least in the traditional sense. It promotes anxiety, and is just plain *boring*. You'll never hear the term from me again because traditional budgeting is associated with deprivation, which serves only to set us up for failure. I want you to think of it as a simple and fun way to *choose* how you want to spend your hard-earned money. Think of why you want to save money: Are you looking to retire, send your kids to college or take a vacation? Is it something you're really excited about or is it just another thing that you think you have to do? Instead of thinking of retirement as a vague notion that is years away, think of how you're going to be spending your retirement. Will you travel the world? Own a beachfront cottage? Volunteer for a favorite cause? How would you spend your time if you didn't have to work for a living? We've put lots of emphasis on building dreams in previous chapters so think of your spending plan as putting your dreams into action.

Your Daily Cash Tracker is designed to make you aware of all the little nooks and crannies into which you pour money mindlessly or needlessly. You can analyze it and determine what's a necessity, what's reality and what's got to go. Your spending plan is for progressing toward your dreams. Tracking will coincide with your monthly spending plan, but ultimately the tracker is to help you refine your habits over the next 90 days.

If you're feeling frustrated and overwhelmed, you're not alone. Remember that *Monkey Mind* will return – you just need to remember your positive affirmations and the volume knob that will quell that voice!

Take a few minutes every month to prepare your spending plan. Use the form on the next page for the first month to determine what you're currently spending and what you want to spend. At the end of the month, enter what you actually spent from your cash tracker. When you put together the spending plan for your second month, move the *actual* column from your first month to the *current* column for your second month so you can compare and improve.

Think of the diet-plan adage "a moment's pleasure on your lips, a pound of fat upon your hips." If you look at it from a dollar-a-pound standpoint, the moment's pleasure of purchasing a $4.00 magazine you don't need and don't even read all the way through turns into a 200 pound blob of fat on your financial body. Who wants *that*? The few minutes you spend tracking your expenses each day are the push-ups and tummy-tucks of your financial health.

Once you've finished your first month's plan, you'll have some solid ground on which to stand in moving forward. And that, my friend, is the subject of our next chapter – Diva Debt in Perspective.

Spending Plan • Month of:

EXPENSE	CURRENT	NEW	ACTUAL
Mortgage/Rent			
Telephone			
Utilities			
FOOD			
Groceries			
Restaurant			
Other			
ENTERTAINMENT			
Movies			
Video Rental			
Concerts			
Music CD's			
Books			
Miscellaneous			
AUTOMOBILE			
Loan/Lease Payment			
Insurance			
Repairs			
Gasoline			
Maintenance			
Miscellaneous			
CLOTHING			
Work Clothes			
Casual Clothes			
Special Event Clothes			
Dry Cleaning			
GIFTS			
PERSONAL CARE			
Skin Care Products			
Hair Care Products			
Makeup			
Hair Cuts / styling			
OTHER ITEMS			

CHAPTER 9
DIVA DEBT IN PERSPECTIVE

*"If you want greater prosperity in your life,
start forming a vacuum to receive it."*

Catherine Ponder

CHAPTER 9 • DIVA DEBT IN PERSPECTIVE

DIVA SPEAK:
I am responsible with my debt and keep it in perspective.

Oblivia knew she was in debt but had no idea how deeply or in what way, holding only to being "in debt," and getting nowhere despite making monthly payments. One day her friend Prospera spoke cheerfully about her upcoming college graduation and the payments on her student loan, saying it was the "best debt" she ever incurred. Oblivia was surprised to learn that there are different kinds of debt, and she decided to analyze her situation. She was paying off several credit cards, a car loan and a student loan. Her student loan had a low interest rate and if she hadn't borrowed money to attend college, she wouldn't be as happy in her career as she is today. And if she hadn't borrowed the money for the car she couldn't get to work! She realized the cost of her education and automobile provided her with a real advantage and the debt she owed for them was not bad. Oblivia decided to concentrate on the *ugly debt* – the credit card balances – while making minimum payments on the others. Putting her debt into perspective brought Oblivia to an acknowledgement that she really did have a handle on her situation; within a few months her progress was obvious, and the last we heard she was only a few thousand dollars away from the down payment on a new home.

WHAT IS DEBT

Debt is often a necessary part of our everyday lives, and our hopes and dreams. If we need a student loan to pay for college, or a car loan in order to get to work, it is *necessary* debt. Unfortunately, when we let it get out of control it becomes a train wreck looking for a crooked track. Having more bills than money causes stress and anxiety, particularly in a society that encourages us to spend and buy on credit – digging us deeper in debt. The plain and simple truth is that you can't expect things to change unless you take different action with your money habits. It's like riding a bike. Once you learn and practice the easy techniques to eliminate debt and free up money, they'll become second nature. Remember, what you think about you talk about, and what you talk about you bring about. For good or for bad, your current beliefs about money have served you in some way. Every financial challenge can be overcome, no matter how hopeless you believe it is. So let's learn about the different types of debt, put it into perspective and take immediate action to eliminate it!

GOOD DEBT

There is such a thing as good debt! Typically, it is incurred as an investment on items that have a good chance of increasing in value – a home mortgage, for example. If you buy a $100,000 home, borrowing $90,000 and putting $10,000 down, you have $10,000 equity, which is considered an asset. A year later, your home is worth $105,000. Your equity has risen to $15,000, plus the principal you paid that year. Your $10,000 investment has grown to $15,000 – a 50% return on your investment, which would not have taken place had you not borrowed $90,000 in the first place. College loans are another example of good debt, as you are investing in your future and hopefully your future income potential.

BAD DEBT

Bad debt is incurred in the purchase of something that will decrease in value. It may be something that you need – a car or an appliance – but the minute you drive that car off the lot or plug in your washing machine, it's worth far less than what it cost. If you must finance the purchase of a car – most people do – make sure you know what you're paying for, and how much it will cost over the long haul. You'll find lots of seductive deals out there – you just need to figure out which one works for you.

UGLY DEBT

Ugly debt is – you guessed it – typical credit card debt. Dinners out, clothes, entertainment and other unconscious spending really add up once you have the convenience of pulling out that plastic. Unless you are paying off your credit card every month, these purchases end up costing you plenty in the long run – especially if you are only making minimum payments. Consider this: credit card companies normally require a minimum payment of only 3% of the balance. A $3,900 balance at 18% would take nearly 42 years to pay off, and cost a total of $14,530.44 – short term gain, long term pain! Imagine taking 42 years to pay off things like dinners, outfits or compact discs. Your only dream would be that you owned the credit card company! Keep a credit card for *emergencies* – and just having to have that designer dress or drinks with a buddy after work do *not* qualify as emergencies – and use a debit card for all other expenses. When you spend, at least you know that you've got the money to pay for it now, not 42 years from now. Think of it this way: *Do you want to pay full price plus interest for used goods?* Ugly debt fuels a lifestyle and creates poverty that you don't yet feel. It fulfills whims of immediate gratification at the expense of your dreams.

WHEN YOU FEEL THE URGE TO SPLURGE...

Print the questions below onto a 3x5 card or a sheet of paper you can carry in your pocket or purse. Each time you consider making a credit card purchase, pull that card out and think about the questions before you whip out that piece of plastic. When you spend unconsciously, you'll have the credit card debt to show for it.

1) Do I need this item right now? Is this a *need* or a *want*? Big difference between the two!
2) How am I feeling right now? Am I stressed or upset about something in my life?
3) How will I feel when I look at my credit card statement and need to pay for this item?
4) What is missing in my life that I am trying to fill by making this purchase?
5) Will this purchase improve the quality of my life a year from now?

Answer these questions truthfully every time the desire to whip out your credit card arises, and you'll realize the immediate gratification you experience may not be worth the regret you'll feel later. Use these questions to "buy" yourself some time so you can put spending in perspective.

EMOTIONAL DEBT

Our negative feelings about ourselves are *emotional* debts that prevent us from living with E.A.S.E. and moving toward our dreams. The feelings of inadequacy, shame, blame and resentment we experience stifle the vibrant energies that create more time and money. Interestingly, it can be our emotional debt that creates and keeps us in financial debt. To rid ourselves of emotional debt is to improve our self worth, which in turn eliminates our financial debt and increases our net worth.

SET THE STAGE

Progress – not perfection – that's what we're after, particularly when it is easy to be paralyzed with the reality of debt. We move through stages as we progress, and we need to honor ourselves in each one. Consider the following stages of debt and decide where you fit. There's no such thing as *good or bad, right or wrong* when determining what stage you are in at the moment. The most important thing is to tell the truth and realize that the goal is to end up at Stage 6 – the Revival Stage – having learned your lesson, achieved a sense of self-confidence, and paid your debt!

Stage 1: **Denial** – You still feel good. You've attained an "artificial high" after making some purchases, but have mounting debt to show for it. Your bills are growing, but you have basically denied that they exist and refuse to deal with the situation.

Stage 2: **Upset** – You're upset about your debt. You're angry with yourself or with another party for helping you get into this mess. Blame and shame reside here.

Stage 3: **Dejected** – You feel hopeless, thinking that your debt will never go away. It's hard to rise from this stage when you have such negative emotions. This is a time when it's important to keep revisiting positive beliefs and affirmations and look at your list of *100 Things*.

Stage 4: **Juggler** – In this stage you rob Peter to pay Paul. You say to yourself, "I can pay off Loan A at the expense of Loan B" or "I'll pay off this credit card with another credit card." You are trying to solve the problem with a quick fix and end up just moving your debt around – not taking the necessary steps to get rid of it. These are *Band-Aid tactics* instead of *long-term solutions*.

Stage 5: **Embrace** – At this stage you see your debt for what it really is and embrace the fact that you can do something about it. Why? Because you're willing and have sought help by reading this book. You are willing to tell the truth. Every step you take moves you closer to your dreams. From this point forward, there's nowhere to go but up!

Stage 6: **Revival** – Self Confidence lives here. You've put your debt into perspective and learned your lessons. You've started an introspective journey and are paying down your debt in a systematic way. Debt is now your servant and not your master. Look how far you've come!

WHERE DO YOU FIT TODAY?

Analysis Paralysis, or the constant examination and analyzation of your current stage can be used as an excuse to avoid positive action. What this is really about is being aware of which stages you tend to get stuck in and take the necessary steps to free yourself from the repetitive rut by creating new beliefs and habits!

DEBT ELIMINATION

You've got 2 choices:
1) *SPEND LESS*
2) *EARN MORE*

For most people this makes logical sense but these choices aren't always easily put into action. Beyond the intellectual knowledge of what needs to happen, we have to deal with the subconscious causes of our behavior. Spenderfella, a compulsive spender, won't last long in a no-spending zone, because he has not first been willing to determine the root of his *need* to spend.

Imagine you're in a pool of water, surrounded by beach balls, each representing a character trait or habit you'd like to change. When you push a ball under the water, you can only hold it there so long before you have to use your hands to stay afloat. The minute you let go, that ball pops right back up to the surface, and probably splashes you in the face. If, however, you knew where the air inlet was for that ball, and were able to release it, the ball would simply deflate.

Here's what you need to eliminate bad and ugly debt once and for all:
- Commitment – to not incur more bad or ugly debt.
- Discipline – to stick to the plan, which won't be hard once you see how quickly your debt decreases.
- Imagination – to be able to feel what your life will be like without the burdens of debt. Here is where your dreams and your "100 Things" list comes in!

Practical strategies that others have found useful:
- Place your credit cards in a container of water and freeze them. You'll probably lose the urge to spend in the four hours it takes for them to thaw out.
- Shop without credit cards and use your debit card for convenience.
- Don't use any items that you paid for by credit card for at least a week. You'll have an additional week to evaluate your purchase – and possibly return it.
- If you absolutely must use a credit card, immediately write a check in the amount you charged and deduct that amount from your bank account balance.

Will there be slip-ups? Yes, but what's important is that you get right back on your journey.

YOUR DEBT-ELIMINATION PLAN

Grab a pencil, some paper and a list of all your debts. We're going to create your personal debt-elimination plan, and I promise that when you have this all down on paper, you'll feel *better*, not *worse*. You've come a long way already, and should recognize that from this point, your debt is going to go down, while your net worth and spirits go *up*.

Step 1: Make a list of your debts, starting with the smallest balance. Most financial planners believe it's important to start with the debt carrying the highest interest rate. But I feel it's important to see progress – and paying off a debt in full builds excitement and the momentum to continue.

Debt	Amount	% Rate	Minimum Payment	Margin Amount	Total Payment

Step 2: Determine how much cash you were able to free up from Chapter 9 – we'll call this your "margin money" – and write that number in the space below. Some participants choose to turn this exercise into a game – a race to see how quickly they can get to the *debt-free finish line*. Imagine yourself as an athlete, racing against your debt – your goal, your Olympic Gold Medal, is the day you reach "0" in the Debt column – and your competition is that piece of plastic in your wallet.

Step 3: Be prepared to pay the minimum amount required each month for all your bills. Pay the minimum amount PLUS your margin money on the bill with the lowest balance. For example, if the minimum payment is $25 and you found $100 of margin money, your payment would be $125.

Step 4: Once your first bill is paid, take the total payment you were making against it – in our example it was $125 – and add that amount to the minimum payment you were making on the second bill on the list. Continue on down the list and watch how quickly your debt disappears!

Step 5: Always be thinking of new ways to free up money so you can increase your margin number. Tracking your expenses should help. You can also include bonus money or raises to really speed up the process!

Step 6: Add up the money you'll have available to invest as your debts disappear. Write that number here:

To show the tremendous effects of compounded interest, $300 invested every month at a rate of 8%* equates to more than $250,000 in 25 years time. You will have saved over a quarter-million dollars – how big will your dreams be then?

*8% may or may not be attainable, it's being used here only as an example.

A NOTE ON BANKRUPTCY

Before the availability of credit cards, we couldn't compensate for personal inadequacies by spending money. When it comes to getting into financial trouble, people haven't changed, but our environment definitely has. In the 1940's, you couldn't buy a new outfit without cash in hand. Today, we whip out plastic without a moment's thought – and bankruptcy rates have skyrocketed. We become overwhelmed and despondent when bills outweigh our income, and sometimes we think bankruptcy is the only way out.

There are alternatives to bankruptcy. If you find yourself in a position where bankruptcy appears the only solution, please take the time to explore other options. Filing bankruptcy puts a negative mark on your credit rating, and will prevent you from obtaining new credit for a minimum of two years *assuming* you are able to keep up with income taxes, utilities and other payments.

- Determine areas where you can free up cash. Expenses for food, toiletries, clothing, gas and miscellaneous items usually have the most room for adjustment.
- Can you create additional sources of income to increase your cash flow? Taking on odd jobs, or securing a part-time weekend position are two ways you can increase cash flow, and there are many other creative endeavors you can explore.
- Have you communicated with all your creditors to discuss the creation of an acceptable payment plan. Most creditors are willing to work with you to structure a plan that fits within your income and assures them of payment, as they lose the chance of recovering any funds at all if you file for bankruptcy.

Although bankruptcy is sometimes the only option, it's important to honor our debts for our own sake, and for the sake of those to whom we owe the money. Honoring our debts clears the road for us to move into the real task of our money relationship – funding our dreams.

CHAPTER 10
FUND THE DREAM

*"All things are possible until they are proved impossible –
and even the impossible may only be so, as of now."*

Pearl S. Buck

CHAPTER 10 • FUND THE DREAM

DIVA SPEAK:
I am open and receptive to learning about investing for my future with E.A.S.E.

Dear **Feartensia**:

I've been thinking about our conversation yesterday and want to tell you more about what I'm doing to have funds set aside for retirement. Just like you, I didn't have the vaguest idea about investing, and only a foggy idea of how much money I would need to save, but I was excited to get started, so I attended an investment seminar. It sure opened my eyes! All the work I have done lately in tracking my expenses and spending habits has paid off, so to speak, because I found ways to free up $500 every month, which I am using as the basis for my dream account. In the seminar, I learned that $500 per month, invested at an 8% return rate for the next twenty years, will give me more than $275,000 by the time I am ready to retire and live my dream! Can you imagine? I'll give you all the information on the seminar when we meet for coffee next Thursday. When you're ready to attend the seminar yourself, I'll go with you, and then we can work together to plan *your* investment strategy.
Love,
Prospera

SOMETHING IS BETTER THAN NOTHING

Investing is much like the proverbial race between the tortoise and the hare. One went full tilt right from the gate, then burned out well before the finish line. The other took one measured step at a time, maintaining consistent energy and reaching the goal without exhaustion.

The hare was caught up in thinking he needed to get ahead quickly, so he barreled off at top speed. He was like the person who invests money in a risky stock, makes a bundle, and then loses everything when the stock drops, or the one who commits to putting aside an unrealistic amount and stops investing altogether because the monthly payment is too high.

The tortoise, on the other hand, took the time to understand the hills, valleys, twists and turns of the race track, and measured his energy step by step. He knew where he wanted to end up, and kept moving forward until he crossed the finish line. He was like the person who consistently invests $20 per month, knowing that as he came closer to his goal of being debt-free, the amount would increase. He was in it for the long-term gains.

Something is better than *Nothing*. After you've paid your debt, invest consistently each month. That voice telling you to wait for the "big hit" – the lottery, an inheritance, the Prize People at your door – is *Monkey Mind*, bound and determined to keep you back.

Remember that it's the combination of *head* and *heart* that makes for a positive relationship to money. The head calculates *how much* we need to get there, and *how* we get there. The heart knows *why* investing is important, and keeps our investment strategy in line with our values. If we use one to the exclusion of the other, the result is disastrous. All too often, we hear a great stock tip, let our emotions take over, and fail to do the research that qualifies the stock. Your investments are meant to grow, and they are meant to *serve you*. Never fall in love with a stock, or you'll be Mr. Hare, totally exhausted and sound asleep halfway through the race. When you choose to be the tortoise, you will become wealthy through solid, consistent investing.

TAKE CONTROL!
If you start investing and have to go off your plan temporarily, commit to starting back up as quickly as possible. Take Control – don't let temporary circumstances destroy the permanence of your dreams.

Actually, the process of investing is the easy part – keeping our emotions in line is usually the most difficult aspect. In this chapter, I've outlined the basics of investing and the things you need to know in order to build your confidence and create a plan so simple you'll actually look forward to investing each month.

MOCK IT UP
While you are paying off your debts and learning about investments, create a mock portfolio – pick three or four target investments and *pretend* you have the funds to invest. Understand why you chose them, and watch how they rise and fall on the daily market listings. Pay attention to trends – some industries rise and fall as regularly as the tide but maintain a consistent growth, while another is subject to huge spikes and dangerous crashes. By the time you are ready to begin investing your own funds, you should have a reasonable understanding and won't be taking a total shot in the dark with your money.

KEYS TO INVESTING
Here's what you need:
- consistency
- simplicity
- clarity
- knowledge
- willingness

1) **Consistency:** Are you regularly investing a certain percentage or dollar figure each month? If you fall off track for a month, do you get right back on the following month?
2) **Simplicity:** Is your investment strategy simple enough for you to direct? Do you want to be reading the financial news, watching the financial shows and trying to pick your own stocks? Or do you want to put your money into something that has historically done well? Investing can be as simple or as complicated as you choose to make it. At a dinner party you may

hear others bragging about their stocks or making predictions about the market. Don't let your Monkey Mind tell you that you're not doing enough. If you have a simple philosophy of consistently investing over time, your money will grow.

3) **Knowledge:** Do you know where your money is going? Do you have some basic knowledge of the investment world? See the following section for some simple terminology.

4) **Clarity:** Are you clear on where you are and where you need to go in order to live your dreams?

There are two basic schools of thought when it comes to investing. The first recommends the following order:
- pay off all debt, including your student loans and car payments
- build a reserve account for emergencies
- start investing for the future

The second, more traditional method recommends a different order:
- invest first – pay yourself
- pay off debt simultaneously
- build a reserve account for emergencies

I recommend a middle-of-the-road scenario, which is outlined later in this chapter.

This is not a book about investing, as there are many resources you can tap to round out your knowledge. As you're learning, I recommend you read financial publications, visit web-sites or watch the financial news. This will help you become familiar with the terminology and give you more confidence. There are many places to start, including web-sites that will calculate how much money you will need to invest for retirement, to save for college or whatever your dreams may be.

SIMPLE TERMINOLOGY

Here is some simple terminology you should know to help get you started:

Allocation: The monies you set aside for a particular investment.

Appreciate: When the value of your investment goes up.

Bond: A loan you are making to a bond seller who promises to pay it back within a specific time period and with a specific amount of interest. They are issued by both corporations and the government. Some bonds pay interest in specific intervals, with the principal being repaid at maturity, while others pay back both the interest and the principal on the maturity date.

Certificate of Deposit (CD): A form of bond that has very low risk and can be bought in varying amounts – usually starting at $100. Typically, the larger the amount and the longer time to maturity, the higher interest rate earned.

Compound Interest: Interest calculated not only on the initial principle, but also on the accumulated interest of prior periods. In other words, you're earning interest on your interest.

Depreciate: When the value of your investment goes down.

Diversification: A strategy designed to reduce exposure to risk by combining a variety of investments, such as stocks, bonds, real estate and cash – which are unlikely to all move in the same direction.

D.R.I.P. Plans: Plans that allow you to buy stock directly from companies, free of any brokerage commission and often in amounts as low as $10 per month. Doesn't seem like much, but a great way to start investing for anyone who has less than $500. Remember, every dollar makes a difference!

401-K: A tax-deferred retirement fund set up by corporations for employees. Typically, employers match employee contributions by varying percentages. The money is invested in a variety of vehicles – stocks, bonds, CD's and is not taxed until it is withdrawn at retirement age. What's great about 401K's or other company plans is that you can have your monthly contribution automatically taken out of your paycheck. The Canadian equivalent is known as RRSP – Registered Retirement Savings Plan.

Dollar cost averaging: An investment strategy designed to reduce volatility in which money is invested in fixed dollar amounts at regular intervals, such as once a month, regardless of what direction the market is moving.

Index: An unmanaged selection of stocks or bonds whose collective performance is used as a standard to measure investment results. Examples: Dow Jones Industrial Average, Standard & Poors 500, The Wilshire 5000.

Index Fund: A mutual fund that seeks to match the performance of a particular market index. Partially due to lower expenses, index funds outperform the majority of actively managed mutual funds.

Individual Retirement Account (IRA): A retirement account where individuals can contribute up to $3000 (in 2003) per year and receive tax breaks. (The number is growing and will be even higher in coming years.)

Keogh Plan: A tax-deferred pension plan, similar to the ones listed above for employees of unincorporated business or for the self-employed.

Liquidity: Determines how readily accessible money is.

Money Market: A generally safe, liquid investment.

Mutual Fund: Money from individuals and institutions that is pooled by an investment company to invest for a fee. One share of a mutual fund can actually be invested in hundreds of individual companies. Mutual funds have different philosophies – some simply track the general market, others invest in high-risk ventures and others invest in certain market sectors such as technology or health care.

Pension Plan: A retirement plan established by employers, unions, governments, etc. There are many different types, so if your employer offers one it is important to understand how your particular plan works.

Risk tolerance: How much risk are you willing to tolerate? If you're aware and comfortable with the fact that the over time, the stock market will consistently grow, but that there will be peaks and valleys along the way, then you should put a larger portion of your money into stocks. If, on the other hand, stocks make you nervous and you can't stomach the ups-and-downs, you should probably have a larger portion of your money in bonds or fixed assets.

Roth IRA: A retirement plan where contributions are made with after-tax dollars, but all contributions and earnings are tax-free if withdrawals are made after age 59 1/2.

Rule of 72: A quick formula used to determine how long it will take for an investment to double using a particular rate of return. The answer is determined by dividing the interest rate into 72. For example, if you invested $10,000 at 8%, it would take approximately 9 years for your $10,000 to double to $20,000 (72 divided by 8 = 9.)

Stock: A share of stock gives you partial ownership of the company. As a shareholder, you are entitled to part of the company profits, through dividends. The share price typically rises and falls and is generally based on company, industry and market conditions, trends and forecasts. Ideally, it's best to buy stocks if you will not need the money for at least 5 years. In other words, if you will need the money for a home or for a child's college education within the next 5 years, investing that money in the stock market may be too risky.

Traditional IRA: Money is tax deductible in the contribution year, based on certain income and age restrictions and is withdrawn after age 59 1/2. Earnings are taxed at the regular rate.

UNDERSTANDING RISKS AND RETURNS

Medium Risk Investments – Greater risk and greater potential for return
   Growth Mutual Funds
   Common Stock
   Real Estate
Low Risk Investments – Lower risk and lower potential for return
   Balanced mutual funds
   High grade corporate bond and municipal bond funds
Savings – Very low risk and very low potential for return
   Savings Accounts
   Government savings bonds and treasury bills
   Certificates of deposit
   Money market accounts

YOUR DREAM RETIREMENT

The word *retirement* used to conjure up one strong image for me – sitting on my porch at age 65, busily knitting a sweater and waiting for my grandchildren to visit. Today's retirement, or the *new retirement* is very different and represents many different lifestyles: simply making a career change, working part-time, volunteering, traveling the world or sitting on that porch are all common ways that today's retirees want to spend their time. And many people don't retire at the magical age of 65. Some want to retire at 50 and others can't ever see themselves retired – even at 80. And the money that many of us will spend in retirement will come from different places than previous generations. Social Security is now viewed as only a portion of our retirement nest egg. As pensions are increasingly being replaced by 401-K plans, we are now given more freedom to control our own destiny! The number of women who will be reliant on social security as their only source of income is startling. It's so important for you to put yourself first and create your dream retirement.

As I mentioned in the *Keys to Investing* section, there are two basic schools of thought on the order in which you pay off debt, invest and build your reserve account. Here is a third way that many of my workshop participants have found easy to understand and use*:
1) Contribute the maximum allowable into your company 401-K or Keogh plan that will get a full company match. I actually recommend you invest here before paying off all your debts – but if you're paying high interest rates on your cards, it's your choice to make. Why do I recommend this? The bottom line is that getting the company match is like getting free money. If your company matches up to 6% of your contribution, make sure you are contributing that 6% and double your investment! Your contribution is automatically deducted from your paycheck and it will actually reduce your taxable income. If you've already started investing in your company 401-K plan or Keogh plan – congratulations! If not, why not? Many of us think that when we get that next raise or that next promotion, then we'll start contributing, but that point never seems to come and it's too easy to spend the money. This is the first and most important step in saving for your retirement. Check with your human resources department to find out all of the details on how to set up your 401-K and when you can start contributing. If you are self-employed or don't work for a corporation, the Keogh plan offers similar tax incentives, so find out how you can open up that account from a broker.
2) Pay off all *bad* and *ugly* debt.
3) With additional funds, open up a money market account and contribute every month until you've accumulated 3-6 months of living expenses. This is your reserve account and needs to be easily accessible.
4) If you have additional money to invest, open up a Roth IRA. In 2003 the maximum allowable was $3000 per person per year, and it is going up from there. The beauty of the Roth IRA is that all earnings are tax-free if you withdraw them after age 59 1/2.
5) With even more money to invest, return to your 401-K account and contribute any additional money that won't receive a

match. This money is still tax-deferred until age 59 1/2 and will lower your taxable income this year.
6) Any additional money should be invested in a non-retirement account for your dreams. You will need to open up a standard brokerage account. With a discount broker, you know what stocks, bonds or mutual funds you want to invest in and you will pay a lower fee. With a full-service broker, you will receive investment advice and pay a higher fee. Research different brokers and determine what will meet your unique needs.

*These guidelines are recommended for most people, but please consult a financial adviser to discuss your individual needs.

EGGS AND BASKETS

Other than your money market account, you will have choices to make regarding where your money will be invested within these different vehicles. My best advice here is *Don't put all your eggs in one basket.* You will also need to determine your tolerance for risk and your willingness for learning about investing beyond the basics. Some people are risk takers and have a hunger to learn *sophisticated or advanced* investment methods. Others aren't risk takers at all and have no interest in learning the details of investing. Either type is fine as there are investments and strategies for both categories. Your 401-K will typically offer specific funds for you to choose from. In your IRA and standard brokerage account, you will have unlimited choices of mutual funds, individual stocks, bonds, etc. It's also important here to determine your risk tolerance. If you have 30-plus years until retirement and can weather the market ups and downs, perhaps you will want a higher percentage of your money in stocks. If you're just three years from retirement, you should probably invest in more bonds and fixed assets. Again, find out the risk level of your fund choices and decide if that fits with your objectives. The bottom line is *if you're spending your precious life energy worrying about your investments, you need to change your strategy.*

Choose an advisor you like and trust, and who understands your current situation and your goals. Someone who will help you handle your money as if it were their own, with the respect and integrity that you deserve. Find out in advance how they are paid. It can be either through a flat fee based on a percentage of your investments or by commission based on products sold to you. The only caution I give to you is that when working with an advisor who is paid on commission, be sure that you intuitively know this person has your best interest at heart, rather than selling you products based on their own commission goals.

On a final note, you must be clear, committed and excited for your dream retirement plan to work. Contrary to popular myth, investing for your future can be fun and it can be simple. Remember to undertake this with E.A.S.E.

CHAPTER 11
ORDER, ORDER

"A woman must have her own money
if she is to be truly her own woman."

Germaine Greer

CHAPTER 11 • ORDER, ORDER

DIVA SPEAK:
I am the CEO of my financial life, focused on
Creating Extraordinary Outcomes.

With six maxed-out credit cards in her wallet, **Spenderella** was drowning in debt; her outstanding balances exceeded $12,000. She sometimes left her mailbox unopened for weeks, feeling numb and frozen at the thought of the bills inside. On a particularly frigid day, Spenderella took a nap, and in her dream she saw herself encased in a block of money-colored ice. A fairy godmother came out of nowhere, pulled her from the ice, and placed all her credit cards there instead, saying "Freeze your debt, not yourself." When she woke, Spenderella cancelled all her credit cards, retaining one for emergencies, but froze it in a plastic bag full of water. Her friend Prospero introduced her to a loan officer, who consolidated all her debts into one loan, with only a 12% interest rate instead of the 18% on the credit cards. Spenderella began using her debit card for purchases, and paid as much as she could each month towards the loan. Within eighteen months, Spenderella was a DEBT-FREE DIVA!

GET YOUR HOUSE IN ORDER

It's frustrating when our home is in disarray and we can't find what we're looking for. The same is true with our finances. When we can account for our money and know exactly what we have or don't have in our financial life – we know where we've been and where we need to go. We feel in control and at ease. For most people this is a foreign concept.

Paying attention to detail is the key to maintaining order in our financial life. When we take time in each moment to pay attention to the specifics of our financial life, we avoid doubling up on work later on. How many times have you visited the ATM, withdrawn $40 and forgot to record it in your ledger? Or spent an hour trying to find a bank statement? Or not known how much money is in your checking account? When we play the Scarlet O'Hara role, telling ourselves "I'll think about it tomorrow," we end up spending twice as much time and energy, leading to further frustration.

Think of yourself as the CEO of a cool company called **My Moneyworks, Inc.** You are in the business of creating and enjoying all the time and money to live your dreams. As a CEO, your primary responsibility is have all your financial information in order, knowing exactly where you stand so that you can:

Create
Extraordinary
Outcomes

COUNTING YOUR CASH

Do you know how much cash you have with you at any moment? Is it scrunched up in your pocket, or stuffed in six different pockets? Keep your cash in your wallet, laid neatly in numerical order, facing in the same direction. We feel better when our money is orderly and it's one less thing to be stressed out about. Respect your money by keeping it neat and orderly; respect your money and the universe gives you more!

AUTOMATIC TRANSACTION MANAGEMENT

When we withdraw cash from the ATM, or use our debit card to make a purchase, it's easy to forget what we spent it on, or we forget to record it altogether.

- Each time you withdraw cash, get a receipt, and write "record" across the top.
- Each evening, empty your pocket or purse, and enter the withdrawal or expense in your ledger.
- Put a check mark on the receipt so you know you've recorded the transaction. Letting it go until you get your bank statement

means more headaches since you're now trying to make sense of an entire month of transactions.
- Once you've recorded it in your ledger, place the receipt in your *receipt file*.
- Toss your ATM receipts after you get your bank statement each month.

I became very disciplined with this process because I was often scared at the end of the month, not knowing the balance in my bank account or if certain checks would clear. When I know for certain exactly how much money is available in my account at any given time, I feel more in control, which builds my level of confidence and ultimately I make better choices. To this day, I continue to be conscious of how much money I have available for my spending plan. And when I feel out of control, I have usually let my habit of accounting for my money go by the wayside. Immediately getting back on track is my remedy for taking back positive control.

REMINDER BINDER
I keep my favorite exercises from this book in a special binder for easy access and to remind me of my dreams and goals. Keep your binder light and happy. Create a cover that puts a smile on your face, including pictures of your dreams, your loved ones, keywords and phrases that inspire you. I keep my daily cash trackers and daily journals in my binder and I make a copy of my "100 Things" to look at daily. Choose the exercises or other information that will inspire you and the ones that you want to look at on a regular basis.

FILING SYSTEM
Keep all your financial information accessible and in one location. If you don't have a filing system that works for you, here's what I recommend:
- Determine where you want to keep your files. There's no need to purchase an expensive filing cabinet. Most office supply stores sell boxes that hold hanging file folders.
- Purchase a set of standard manila file folders and a set of hanging file folders with plastic label inserts.
- Use the hanging folders for all of your categories – credit cards, banking, investments, mortgage, will, household bills, insurance, etc.

- Use the individual folders to label each individual item – each credit card, every bill, every insurance policy, etc.
- Organize your files alphabetically, or whatever works easiest for you and start filing your financial papers.
- Keep your files up-to-date by marking *paid* on every bill after it's been mailed and place it in the appropriate file.
- Keep bills and bank statements and investment statements for at least three years, tax information for at least seven years.

Some people find it helpful to label an additional group of files 1 through 31 – representing the days of the month – and place bills in the file for the date they will be paid. This system can be used for tracking other items – if you wanted to check your credit report at the end of the month, you could write a note to yourself and drop it into the file with that date. You can use this system for all kinds of reminders – even when to mail birthday cards. If this will help you, give it a try. If you know it's something that you won't use, don't. A system is only great if you use it and it works for you.

BANKING

Maintaining order in banking requires that we are aware of our accounts and the manner in which they are set up. Are you happy with the accounts that you have? Are you aware of the services that your bank offers? Are you paying unnecessary fees? Does your bank serve *your needs*? Since banks and their services are constantly changing, shop around and monitor changes in bank services to make sure the packages you've selected best suit your needs. When your banking is in order, you will be confident in knowing that your accounts are set up to *serve you*. I like to think of my bank as *my prosperity palace*, so it's important that I set up a banking house that honors *me*. Do what works *for you*, as long as you are aware of everything you have.

Ideally, you should work toward having accounts set up that serve three different functions – a checking account, a reserve account for emergencies and your dream account. You may not be in a position to start funding all of them *today*, but in the future, if you follow the lessons in this book, you will.

There are many new ways of banking for your consideration, including on-line options. Whatever system makes your financial life easier to manage, allows you to know where you stand at all times and provides easy access to all your financial information, is what you need to set up for yourself. There is no *one right answer* but if your current method is not getting you the results you want, it's time to find a new system and put it into action!

BILL-PAYING

The three most common methods of bill payment are:
- pay bills as soon as they arrive
- postpone payment, then scramble to find the bills, sometimes paying them on time and sometimes paying them late
- don't pay any bills

I offer a fourth approach. First of all, place as many bills as possible on automatic payment. Having the payments withdrawn from your bank account simplifies your life considerably. You must, of course, make sure you record the automatic withdrawals in your check registry. Since bill paying can often be an unpleasant experience, let's create a positive ritual around the task:

1) Pick two times each month to sit down with your bills. I like doing it twice a month since most bills come due at different times and we don't want you to be late with a payment! Pick the 15th and the 30th – or other days that coincide with your paydays.

2) Pick a time and place for your bill paying and create a positive atmosphere there. I often set up at my dining room table. It's best to pick a time when you are alone or uninterrupted. Turn off the phone, the television and perhaps put on some music that you enjoy, light candles or burn incense. No doubt, Monkey Mind is chattering at you loud and clear right now! The point is to create an enjoyable and relaxing setting that will help turn this *not-so-enjoyable* task into something a bit more palatable.

3) When a bill comes in, don't panic and don't pay it right away. Don't even open it! Place it in a designated file and return to it on the date you picked.

4) On your designated date, pick up your bills, your checkbook, a pen, calculator, and a wastebasket and go to your newly created *pleasant* place.
5) Open your bills, one at a time, and review them. Make sure you're breathing! This isn't about beating yourself up over what you spent. This is to make sure they are all correct – that all the bills are truly what you owe. On larger bills, like rent or a mortgage, it may be easier to plan to pay half the amount at one sitting and half at the second sitting so you don't end up short at the end of each month. For example, if your house payment is $1000 per month, and you're paid twice a month, you may consider writing a check for $500 (half the house payment) from each paycheck. Essentially what you'd be doing is sending in two checks totaling $1000 while at the same time easing up your cash flow. One of my clients taught me this as she was finding after writing a check for the house payment from one of her paychecks, she was coming up short for other bills and expenses. It's important to immediately record this in your check registry so it will reflect the appropriate account balance. You can figure out the best way to pay your larger expenses based on what days of the month you are paid.
6) Now pay each one, and in the memo write, "With Thanks!" This may sound a little ridiculous, but just try it! I used to *resent* paying my bills until I thought of the bill paying process a little differently. I tended to overlook the fact that a lot of what I was paying was for my own enjoyment. Think of it as a way to allow other people to pay their bills – to be able to do the work they love. Think of the whole process as a team effort and not just about *you*. Giving your thanks is to show appreciation for the fact that you *do* have the money available.
7) When you're finished, stack them up and say "Thanks – I'm grateful that I am able to pay these and happy that others will be able to thrive in their lives." Take a deep breath and congratulate yourself on a job well done! Finally, remember to mail them!

For those of you whose income is based on commissions, or if your paychecks aren't consistent, remember to always maintain *clear communications* with your creditors. The path of least resistance is to avoid the situation – but this can create more anxiety and hardship for you down the road. If you're having trouble paying your bills, it's always better to call your creditors in advance to let them know what's happening and *when* they can expect payment. If you need to set up a repayment plan, do so in a way that you can carry out. Often it's too easy to make promises that cannot be kept. There is honor and integrity in telling the truth and following through with a schedule that allows others to plan accordingly.

CREDIT REPORTS
Your credit report is the financial equivalent of your resume in the employment market. It shows, in great detail, how you deal with money. It's important to check your credit report once or twice each year – more often if you are in the process of a divorce. I'm always amazed at the number of people who haven't seen their credit report in years, or don't realize the importance of checking it on a regular basis. You can request one for free every year by accessing my website at www.debtfreediva.com.

After you've received the report, go through it to make sure *all* the information is correct:
1) Check your name, address, social security number and place of employment. There are many people out there with the same names, so it's important to make sure your information is all about you and not someone else who happens to share your name.
2) Check each trade line. Trade lines are the listings of everything you owe – including mortgages, car loans, student loans and all credit cards. Check all the account numbers and balances to make sure they are correct. I've seen many instances where this information is outdated or inaccurate.
3) Make sure any blemishes or late payments are accurate. Your credit report is only as good as the information that was entered, and often, mistakes are made.

4) Close any inactive accounts. You may see an old credit card listed on your report that you thought was cancelled, or that you no longer use. If you have too much open credit available, it can affect your ability to get credit.

Two ratings are given. The "R" stands for *revolving* or credit that can be used over and over again. A standard credit card is a good example of a revolving line of credit as you can continue to charge up to a certain limit. The "I" rating stands for *installment*. An installment line of credit is credit that can't be used again. A good example is a mortgage or a car loan. You're simply paying off a loan, and not recharging anything back to that loan.

Every trade line receives either an "R" rating or an "I" rating depending on the account type. The following will appear next to each rating: _x30, _x60, _x90, _x120. In front of one of those categories will be a number indicating how timely you were with your payments. For example, you may see 1x30 – meaning you were late on a payment by 30 days for 1 month. Higher numbers will have a more negative impact on your overall credit rating. The ideal rating is 0x30 throughout your credit report. The higher the number – the lower the rating. Again, ratings are dependent on how timely you pay your bills.

Other aspects considered by lenders:
1) Do you have too much available credit? Having too much can be seen as risky to a lender as your ability to repay several maxed-out accounts may come into question.
2) Has a lender closed your account? Having an account closed by a lender is not good, but closing your own account is fine. The former is referred to as *closed by credit grantor* while the latter is referred to as *closed by account holder*. A lender will ultimately close an account when payments have been consistently late and any communication to set up a repayment schedule has been ignored. One has to really push the limit for a lender to close an account. There are also instances where people have forgotten that accounts have been opened.
3) Are your outstanding balances too high? A lender might not be willing to authorize an additional loan to someone who

already owes too much. How much is too much? It all depends on your income and your previous payment patterns.
4) What is your FICO score? You have three FICO scores – one from each credit bureau. They are a measure of your financial responsibility based on your credit history. A score of 680 – 800+ is considered excellent.

And remember, if you have a blemish on your report, it's not the end of the world. Lenders look at the whole picture and will notice recent improvement patterns, so just continue to make every single payment on time. And know that after seven years, most credit blemishes will drop off.

Order, Order with your credit report means checking it every year, preferably twice a year and knowing that it is accurate. If you were applying for a job, would you leave your resume to chance? Getting a credit report can be scary – but knowing that it is accurate is comforting and can provide peace of mind. When you find an inaccuracy on your report, call the credit bureau reporting agency and have the mistake corrected.

Credit Fraud
We've all heard horror stories about someone stealing a name, an address, a checkbook, a social security card or a credit card. Fraud is on the rise and we need to be aware of it. Fortunately, there are simple steps we can take to try and prevent it from happening and limit the damage if it does happen:
1) The next time you order checks, have only your initials instead of your first name printed on them. In case your checkbook gets stolen, the crook won't know how you sign your name, but the bank will. Never include your home phone number – put your work number, and include a P.O. Box rather than a home address if you have one. And this may seem obvious, but never have your social security number printed on your checks!
2) When you are writing a check to pay your credit card bill, don't include the entire account number on the check. The credit card company only needs the last four numbers. You never know how many hands your check will pass through.

3) Place the contents of your wallet on a copy machine, and make a copy of both sides of each I.D. card, credit card, insurance card – everything. You'll know what you had in your wallet if it gets lost or stolen, and you'll be able to react quickly.

We can't prevent everything, so if your wallet does get stolen, here's what you need to do:
1) Cancel your credit cards immediately. It's much easier if you have a list of all the toll-free numbers handy. Keep it in a safe place where you can find it easily.
2) File a police report in the jurisdiction where it was stolen. Although the police won't be going out looking for your wallet, taking this step shows that you were diligent if an investigation is ever conducted.
3) Call the three national credit reporting organizations immediately to place a fraud alert on your name and social security number. Most people don't think to do this, but placing the fraud alert requires any new credit applications to be verified by you with a phone call. The thief won't be able to open up any new credit card accounts under your name.

Here are the phone numbers you need:
Equifax: 1-800-525-6285
Experian: 1-888-397-3742
Trans Union: 1-800-680-7289

DEBIT AND CREDIT CARDS

The reality in today's society is that it's difficult to get by without a credit card and the lure of plastic is strong. We are often seduced with offers – friendly invitations to build a potentially damaging relationship with *ugly* debt. It looks like free money, but it's just the opposite. Credit cards are big business and they're not going away. The average household credit card balance in 1990 was $2,985, and in 2000 that average jumped to $8,100. The average American household has 11 open lines of credit. Credit cards are a problem, a real epidemic. There are black holes in our lives that need to be filled with something other than spending. Interestingly, the credit cards are not the problem – it's the mindless way we use them.

If you're paying off your balance in full each month – that's terrific! If you're not, let's make it your mission to do so. If you are carrying a balance of credit card debt, I recommend that you only use a *debit card* for your purchases. You will need to have money in the bank for everything you buy until that balance gets paid. Follow Spenderella's example and become a true DEBT-FREE DIVA .

Pay your credit card bills in a timely fashion and keep a separate file for each one.

A final note about credit card companies. Unfortunately, they target college students relentlessly. Many students first learn about money from the credit card companies and it's not good. Most colleges now have monetary arrangements with credit card companies and invite them to their campuses to market to students, alumni and faculty. The colleges receive a flat fee and a percentage of the revenues in exchange for allowing this access – and the fees can run into the millions of dollars. So many college students start their adult life in financial bondage – the combination of credit cards and student loans leave them in a deep hole of debt. It's important to teach your kids about the dangers of debt – before they fill out their first credit card application!

Bottom line: Credit cards are a necessity and only dangerous if we fail to live within our means and use them responsibly.

MORTGAGES

There are numerous how-to books on home buying -you can access **www.debtfreediva.com** for more information. Here are just a few basics you should know if you are currently renting with the intention of purchasing a home:

- Don't buy more house than you can afford. I know this may seem obvious, but often what you can afford and what you actually *want* can present two very different realities when you're out house hunting.
- *Use* your spending plan and determine how much you realistically want to pay. It's nice to own a home, but it's more important to have a life while enjoying your home!
- Buy based on your current income, not based on future pay increases. A prudent strategy is to buy a home based on your *present* income and then use any future pay increases to accelerate the payment of your mortgage or fund your dream account.

Most lenders will allow 28% of your gross household income to be used when determining the amount of mortgage you qualify for. Typical mortgage payments include the following:
Principal – the amount paid toward your loan
Interest – the interest on the loan
Taxes – property taxes
Insurance – home insurance and possibly mortgage insurance

Many lenders also approve up to 36% of household income for mortgage AND other debt. This means that if your debt is over 8% of your household income, it may affect your ability to get credit.

When it comes to keeping your mortgage in order, it's important to always be on time with your payments. Keep a special file for all of your home paperwork and know where you stand with everything. Do you know your interest rate? Do you know when and if you should refinance? Do you know the type of your mortgage? Not all mortgages are 30-years at a fixed rate. How much are you paying toward principal, interest, taxes and insurance? Are you paying mortgage insurance? If so, have you generated enough equity to discontinue paying mortgage insurance? There are many fees and procedures involved with home buying, so please make sure you know how your payments are being applied. Again, there are many resources that can help you through the process. There is a special section on mortgages that you can access on my website: **www.debtfreediva.com**

On the subject of interest rates, be forewarned that just because a coworker or friend got a great, low rate doesn't mean that you'll be getting the same. Mortgage rates are constantly changing, as are the different mortgage programs available. Make certain you have a *trusted advisor* working on your behalf so that you get the best mortgage possible.

For those of you who are renting, don't despair. Home buying isn't for everyone. Ask yourself, "What can I do to get closer to living my dreams? Should I invest my extra money and continue renting?" These are personal decisions that we all have to make for ourselves so spend some time investigating all of your options.

INSURANCE

It's important to know where you stand with your insurance and to have all of your paperwork in your *insurance* file. There are different types

of insurance to consider: *life, health, auto, homeowner's and renter's* are among the most common. There are many educational resources available on insurance policies. Here are some questions to ask yourself when determining what you *have* and what you may *need*:
- Do I need this insurance and is it appropriate for my circumstance? For instance, it may be important to have life insurance if you have dependents, but it may not be necessary if no one is relying on you for financial support.
- Am I adequately insured or over-insured? If a beneficiary needed to collect on a policy, would there be enough?
- What are my deductibles? For auto or home insurance, is it beneficial to increase my deductibles and reduce my payments? Very often, by raising your deductibles, you can free up cash for your prosperity plan!
- Do I know everything there is to know about my policies?

Long term care insurance is also a very important consideration once we reach our 50's. With our aging population, more and more of us are interested in being covered in case we need hospitalization or long term care.

With all of the different types of insurance to consider, it's important to learn all you can and speak to a trusted adviser to determine your needs. You can find out more information on life, health, home, auto and long term care insurance by accessing my web-site at **www.debtfreediva.com**.

WILLS

A will is a legal instrument, usually written but sometimes videotaped, designating the specific distribution of an estate, which includes life insurance policies, investment portfolios, trusts, homes, furnishings, collectibles and any ongoing income. It is important that we designate everything we own in order to avoid costly legal bills or even state intervention. Here are two of the most common reasons we give for not having a will:

1) We don't like to think about death – and by not thinking about it, it won't happen. Obviously, we will all die some day and since we don't get to pick the day, it's important to leave our

loved ones without a financial mess to clean up while they're dealing with a loss. Yes, even if we're *young*.
2) We don't believe we have anything to leave. Everyone has something to leave as a will normally includes personal items that may have sentimental value. Again, a will is about respecting our loved ones enough to not burden them with the task of figuring out what to do with our stuff. Think of your will as making a tough time a little easier on the ones we love. Right down to the details of our funeral.

Revise your will whenever your life circumstances change. With divorce, death, and personal problems many of us need to make changes to our wills and haven't done so.

In addition, a living will and a durable power of attorney are very important parts of an estate plan. They honor your wishes in the event that you become unable to make important life decisions. This can include deciding when to continue or discontinue life support or who will care for your children in the event that you're not able to. Again, think of tending to these matters as a way to respect your loved ones and make it easier on them especially while they may be grieving. There are lots of details involved with wills, estates, living trusts and durable powers of attorneys so please refer to my web-site at **www.debtfreediva.com** for help when you start putting yours together. Make it your #1 priority, and be sure to include your spouse, significant other, children, business partner, other family members or friends, or whoever will need the information to properly act on your behalf. You may amass a fortune all by yourself, but when the time comes to honor your wishes you can't do it alone – it takes two.

CHAPTER 12

IT TAKES TWO

"Do unto others as you would have them do unto you."

The Golden Rule

DIVA SPEAK:
I am always clear and concise in my communication about money.

Every time **Hoardesia** asked her fiancée **Oblivio** about his opinion on their wedding plans, he'd tell her no expense was too great for their special day. Hoardesia didn't agree, and planned a beautiful but frugal wedding. After a lovely but small ceremony, they set off on a honeymoon trip that changed their lives – by the time they returned, they had learned that despite their years of dating and pre-nuptial counseling, they didn't know a thing about each other's style of money management. Hoardesia watched every penny and purchased only what was necessary; Oblivio didn't pay attention to money issues of any kind. Oblivio fell in love with many pretty trinkets on their trip, and would have bought them all. Hoardesia kept the credit cards and checkbook in her locked suitcase, unwilling to purchase anything that wasn't vital to their lives. Soon after the honeymoon, the frustrated couple realized their communication would have to improve if their marriage was going to survive. They learned a technique called "I-Talk," in which neither felt attacked by the other. They held a weekly money meeting, discussed common goals and came to agreement on many of the issues that were giving them trouble. It's still a bumpy ride sometimes, but they know that if they continue working on their communication skills and holding weekly money meetings, they will have the funds and the knowledge of how to use it to live their dreams.

IN THE BEGINNING…
Money issues are the #1 cause of divorce and relationship breakups in the United States. Sadly, differences in money management are too often overlooked when we're considering entering into a long-term relationship, marriage, or other partnership. I don't suggest that you ask to see a credit report before the first date, but there are many things to consider before making a merge. Observe how your prospective partner deals with money *in the beginning*, so there are no surprises later. Begin with these questions:
- Does this person handle money with respect? Is money hoarded, or thrown around without regard? Is money more important than people?
- Does this person speak of money negatively or positively?
- What are their values? What are the items or situations on which they spend their money?

MONEY MERGERS
Money is a challenging issue to deal with on our own, and becomes even more complicated when we involve someone else. Whether it be a love relationship, family situation, friendship or business partnership, when a dispute over money arises our emotions take over, and it's rarely pretty! Typically, there's a breakdown in communication and both parties either become antagonistic, or avoid contact altogether, resulting in bigger problems and no resolution to the money issue. Often, the relationship is permanently damaged or destroyed.

There are solutions to prevent this type of "worst case" scenario. It takes practice; learning to communicate in a respectful manner will help you to achieve *money harmony*.

TYPICAL MONEY MERGERS

Dudes and Divas	Divas and Divas
Dudes and Dudes	Blended Families
Parents and Children	Business Partners
Siblings	Friends

The common thread running through all money mergers is *communication*. Unfortunately, effective communication is one of the hardest things to achieve openly and consistently particularly when money is involved. Yes, it's easy when all is going well – but when the waters get rough and finances are tight, it's a different story – emotions run high, and we resort to speaking with anger, resentment and frustration. Doors slam, inside the house and inside our hearts and minds. The good news is that clear communication is a skill we can develop, with practice. It comes down to a variation of the Golden Rule: *Communicate with others as you would have them communicate with you.* Speak with respect, compassion, understanding, flexibility and a willingness to reach a solution. It's about looking through money – or the ancient Chinese coin – at your relationship with yourself and how that ultimately impacts your relationship with others. The closer matters are to our hearts, the more vulnerable we become.

Years ago, I borrowed money from a dear friend in order to buy a home. The arrangement came together easily and neither of us thought of the *worst case scenario.* Our arrangement was that the monies would be paid back with interest upon the sale of the home and backed up with necessary legal documents. Unfortunately, my circumstances changed and I had to put the home up for sale in an economic climate that gave little possibility for my friend recovering her money. I panicked. Afraid to face the truth, I was riddled with shame, guilt and embarrassment. Monkey Mind reminded me, consistently and loudly, that I was irresponsible. My willingness to communicate with my friend dissolved. She grew frustrated and angry with my lack of communication on how I was planning to resolve the situation and return her money. Sadly, our friendship came to an ugly, bitter end communicated through lawyers. I had lost respect for myself, developed a lack of self confidence and believed that I was a *bad* person because of the mess I had created.

A few years later, through gut-wrenching personal work, I gradually came to forgive myself for past mistakes, contacted my friend with a sincere apology, and offered a repayment solution. It was a monumental step in my life and I felt a clearing of old, outmoded ways – a creation of new energy that allowed me to make great progress toward living my dreams. I am happy to share that our friendship has been rekindled and stands, today, on a stronger foundation.

Unresolved situations hold great power and create feelings of inadequacy; they block our progress. My fears and feelings of inadequacy brought me down, but reinventing my self worth allowed me to bring healing to this situation because I learned the importance of open and truthful communication. The many lessons I learned and the valuable insights I gained were all possible because I used money as the vehicle to look through. And I saw my relationship to myself.

OPENING DOORS
Think about a relationship in your life that has broken down because of money. Perhaps you lent a family member a large sum of money and have yet to be paid back, or as in my story, borrowed money and have not yet found a way to repay the loan. This exercise will begin to release you from the guilt and shame of the situation, and bring clarity to the ways in which you can communicate your concerns clearly and effectively.

1) What situation came to mind?
2) What emotions did you feel as you were writing this down? Where in your body did you feel these emotions?
3) What steps have been taken to resolve this situation?
4) What is the current condition of this relationship? Has the situation been resolved?
5) If it hasn't been resolved, what are you willing to do? What action steps do you need to take? When are you willing to take them?

It's all too easy to feel negative emotions in sticky situations. But without bringing it to resolution, it will continue to absorb your precious energy, and prevent you from creating your dreams. Make sense? I also want to acknowledge that cleaning up a money situation is often uncomfortable. It's easier to avoid conflict than face it head-on, but when we hold on to bitterness and resentment, it's as if our shoes were glued to the floor, and the only way to move is to find the solvent that dissolves the glue without ruining the shoes and burning our feet. Believe me, you'll feel great relief and a rush of positive energy when you resolve your *sticky* situations! Above all, when you've brought resolution to a money issue, remember – you are *not* your past mistakes. Inevitably you will have grown and evolved in your sense of self worth and it's unlikely that you will repeat the negative patterns. Unless *you* choose to.

Here are four important steps that maintain open communication and create resolution:
1) Use clear, concise language. Ask yourself, "Am I speaking in a way I would want to be spoken to?" It's easy to place blame and act defensively; the effect is that we shut down any productive conversation about money. Check your defenses and hurt feelings at the door – enter the discussion with respect and consideration for yourself and the other person, knowing there is no such thing as right or wrong, good or bad – only different opinions that need to be changed to one of mutual understanding and agreement.
2) Practice compassionate listening. Ask yourself, "Am I openly listening to what this person is *really* saying?" Hear the voice inside of you. If you're carrying on an inner dialogue of disagreement with the other person, then you're not *really* listening. Observe your own body language as the other person is speaking. Are your arms and legs crossed? Is your body tense? Are you preplanning what your response is going to be as soon as they finish? Chances are great that if you truly *listen* – if you pay attention to *what* they are saying rather than the emotion in which it is dressed, you will have compassion for their viewpoint, be more understanding of what they need, and make your communications clear, with the intention of finding a solution.
3) Suspend judgments and resentments. This is easier said than done when we're in the middle of an argument, but if you're not willing, chances are the other person won't be, either. Do you like it when others are judging and resenting you? We feel that negative energy coming when we're busy trying to win an argument or dodge bullets – there is no room to solve the problem. Judgments and resentments mask the fact that we're feeling hurt by certain experiences and events. When we get to the truth, much can be resolved. Telling the truth about what's really going on softens our hearts and allows two people to stand together in facing an issue. Using *I-Talk* removes blame and puts *you* in control of your reactions and responses. When you start the conversation with *I feel,* the other person does

not experience *attack*, and will not be defensive because you are, after all, speaking only about your own feelings! Look at two different ways to say the same thing:

Typical response: "You *never* pay back money that you owe – and you're *not* responsible with money. I'm angry at you and I want my money now."

I-Talk: "I'm feeling resentful because you owe me money and haven't paid it back, or come to me with a plan for repayment. I'm hurt, and I don't want to feel this way toward you."

Which response would you be more willing to address?

4) Practice forgiveness. Often the hardest thing to do is to forgive someone who you feel has done you wrong. But the truth is that once you forgive, you free *yourself* to create a solution to your problem. Our voice of the critic doesn't condone forgiveness. It thinks forgiving would mean that we're being doormats and letting people walk all over us, or that that we're out of control in a comparison of right and wrong. Frankly, you will never be able to control or change how the other person has behaved, and to practice understanding and forgiveness is for your benefit. If the tables were turned, would you want someone to forgive you for a perceived wrongdoing or would you want them to continue holding a grudge? Being able to forgive opens up our creative energies to discover productive solutions. Often, our unwillingness to forgive another often occurs in the areas of our own lives where we haven't forgiven ourselves.

THE "I" FACTOR
Me, Myself and I
Re-write the sentences below using *I-Talk*, following the example in Step 3 above. Recite your revisions out loud. These may have nothing to do with your personal situation, but do the exercise anyway! It will help you to communicate more effectively in money matters and in other areas of your life.

Example:
- I'm working hard to save money and you're blowing it all on shopping trips!

  I-Talk: *I'm working hard to save money and when **I see** you spending the money on your shopping trips, **I feel** you're not committed to our financial dreams, and **I'm concerned**.*

  Do you see the difference when you recite it before and after using I-talk?

Now it's your turn!
- That credit card is causing nothing but problems. You need to cut it up!

  I-Talk:

- You're making all the financial decisions and you're leaving me out of everything.

  I-Talk:

THE GOLDEN RULES OF COMMUNICATION

Money communication problems *have nothing to do with the money* in most cases. But two different money personalities will need to work a little harder in order to keep a relationship harmonious! Oblivio and Hoardesia, the couple in our opening story, are a common coupling. Oblivio never pays attention and Hoardesia is basically cheap, hoarding every penny. They fight like this:

Hoardesia: "You make me nuts! Checks are bouncing because you have no idea how much money we have. You spend without knowing how much money is in our checking account and I can't stand it!"

Oblivio: "You never spend a penny and I'm buying things that we need!"

I've come across many different types of money relationship problems, most of which can be resolved with commitment to the following process:

Step 1: Set up regular money meetings. Schedule a meeting once a week that is free of distractions – no kids, no visitors and no phones – not even your cell phone!

Step 2: Take five deep breaths.

Step 3: Allow three to five minutes for each partner to talk about what has been going on regarding finances. If you need to, set a timer. Don't just dive into the problems – talk about what has been working and *then* discuss what could stand improvement using *I-Talk*. Really listen as the other person speaks – with no interruptions, and no judgments. If you find yourself escaping into judgement mode, ask yourself, "Isn't this important enough that we both deserve to be heard?" After one partner finishes their time slot, the other answers back with, "What I heard you say was…" Repeat what was heard using an unemotional, neutral tone – NOT a defensive response. And ask, "Did I get that right?" Then ask, "Is there any more?" Keep going until both parties have said everything they need to say.

Step 4: Now you need to find a common goal – something that brings you both a measure of excitement. Do you have a vacation coming up? Are you saving for a down payment on a house? Spend a few minutes talking about your common goal.

Step 5: Take as long as you need to air your differences and discuss real solutions starting each session with, "I will do my very best to understand your position." The key is for each side to be willing to really listen and understand the other.

Step 6: Schedule your next money meeting and keep practicing your communications skills.

The bottom line is – relationships are all about the golden rule: "Do unto others as you would have them do unto you." So simple, yet so easy to forget. Remember that the stress and anxiety you experience can be prevented or minimized by taking deep breaths and picturing your desired outcome. It's easy to be reactive and defensive yet what you must strengthen is your ability to be proactive and willing to create a solution. Remember that communication is not only what you say, it's also what you don't say, but perhaps what you think. For example, you may be sitting in a defensive body position, thinking negative thoughts toward the other person, while continuing to be polite. The reality is that negative nonverbal communication can be just as damaging to a relationship as a screaming match.

Keep in mind that it's not *really* about the money – it's about the ability to communicate clearly and openly – to hear and be heard. Money matters represent a vehicle to hone communication skills that will affect other areas of your life.

MONEY AND CHILDREN

We all know how important early learning is in all aspects of a child's life – and money is no exception. Give your children guidance to help them create a positive relationship to money early in their lives. What can you do with a 4-year old? The real lesson at any age is to know that money is here to serve us and that the only value it has is that which we place upon it. Here are a few ideas that have worked for other parents:

- Make saving fun. Place a big jar near the door where family members can put loose change at the end of each day. At the end of the summer, all the money in the jar will go toward the family vacation or for another purchase that excites the entire family. It can be fun if every member puts into a box three suggestions for what to do as a family. When it comes time, one suggestion is picked and carried through on. Using jar money to pay the water bill doesn't work and isn't allowed for adults or kids!
- Include the children in family money time each month. Instead of trying to keep them interested in every detail, allow them to hear about your dreams or how you're saving for their college education. Ask them to think about their dreams – they may think twice about asking for that fifteenth doll or toy truck once they start to realize that saving for their education is important!
- When your children reach seven or eight years of age, depending on the child, allot a certain amount of money to cover some of their expenses. Figure out what you would normally pay for such as movies, treats, birthday gifts, or other items. Give

them that amount at the beginning of each month and allow them to be responsible for those expenses. When they get a little older, start adding other items such as clothes to the list. It may take a few months for them to get the hang of it, as they may be tempted to spend it all in the first week – so take it slowly. If they get in a pinch at the end of the month and need a birthday present for a friend, it's OK to let them *borrow* money against a future month – occasionally – as long as they are learning and improving each month.

- I'm a firm believer that kids should earn small amounts of money by doing extra chores around the house, running a lemonade stand or selling old books and toys to a second-hand store. The money they *earn* will have special meaning for them. When I was growing up, I was never given an allowance and I had a different perspective than my friends. My friends had the opportunity to earn, save and make decisions based on what they wanted and what they could afford. Because I literally thought money grew on trees, I never practiced saving the money I had which definitely got me into trouble years down the road. Of course, hindsight is always keener!
- Give your children a set allowance, but divide it up into portions. One portion for savings, one portion for church or charity, and one portion to spend. This will help them learn the importance of saving, giving and even spending responsibly. And let your children pick the charity, so it will have a more personal and lasting impact. These habits introduced in early years will serve them in a positive ways in later years.

Remember the adage – If you give a man a fish, you feed him for a day. If you teach him *to* fish, you feed him for a lifetime. Instilling respect and responsibility for money in your children goes a long way in creating healthy, prosperous money management skills for their adult life. You're teaching them a skill, the value of money, and the value of work and reward.

CHAPTER 13
WORK, WORK, WORK

*"Always be a first-rate version of yourself,
instead of a second-rate version of somebody else."*

Judy Garland

DIVA SPEAK:
I am open to creating a work environment that honors who I am.

Feartensia's bumper sticker said it all: "I owe, I owe, so off to work I go." She saw her job as a receptionist in a law firm as nothing more than a paycheck, an attitude that was apparent to her coworkers and employers. She ate lunch alone every day, while the rest of the staff laughed and joked at another table. One winter day she looked out the window at the clear blue sky and thought "How pretty the snow looks when it sparkles in the sunlight!" Feartensia felt happy with this thought. Returning to her desk, she wrote it down and looked at it several times throughout the afternoon, and added a line – "I'm grateful my desk chair is so comfy!" That night, she started writing in a journal – making note of the things for which she was grateful every day. After a few weeks, she realized that there were many things about her job that she actually enjoyed and that the grass isn't always greener on the other side. She started taking the time to get to know her co-workers and learn about the legal process. She'll be taking her comfy chair with her when she moves into the office reserved for her when she graduates from law school in a few months, and the Partners are all excited about her commitment to the firm and her positive, willing attitude. The bumper sticker, by the way, is long gone.

WHAT IS WORK

It's been said that we're successful when we can't tell the difference between work and play. When we consider how much of our precious life is spent working, it's so important to allocate time to feed our soul. Isn't it uplifting when we see a mail carrier whistling a tune on a sunny day along her route, or a waitress serving us lunch with an infectious smile? Do they know something we don't know?

Typically, "work" is defined as how we make a living. For many people, work is simply *a job*. They don't love it, they don't hate it – it pays the bills and keeps them from financial ruin. The acronym J.O.B. – *Just Over Broke* – portrays an attitude that is guaranteed to create a life in which you are always just a few bucks ahead of *being* broke. It speaks of a comfort zone that may not be entirely comfortable, but is certainly familiar. It is in this place that people usually resist change as the circumstances are not unbearable, and the fear of success is sometimes stronger than the fear of failure. For those of you who have a J.O.B., consider the possibility of exploring your dreams at work.

Ideally, you should be passionate about your career or vocation. When we're excited, enthusiastic and challenged in our work everyday, it doesn't feel like *work* – it begins to be *play*. When we're passionate in life and work, the ripple effect inspires others. Which would you rather have – a boss who is passionate and enthusiastic, or negative and depressing? For that matter, wouldn't *you* rather be someone who is passionate and enthusiastic? When we're passionate, we're creative. We need to state our intentions and tell the universe that we're doing something to make the world a better place.

The exercises in this chapter will help you think of new possibilities. If you already know you're in the perfect line of work, all the better! Keep in mind that many people have a pleasant job that they may not be passionate about – but they pursue their passions outside of the workplace, which is perfectly OK. What we need to avoid is the rut of familiarity. When we're doing what we love, we're more open to prosperity and having the life we say we want.

CHAPTER 13 • WORK, WORK, WORK

DISCOVERING YOUR AUTHENTIC WORK
Part A.
With pen in hand, think about the things you love to do. Forget about money or salary and don't edit yourself. Just let your thoughts and your pen flow – writing how you would spend your time if you knew you would always have all the money you needed to live the life you wanted. Here are some interests others have shared with me: working with youth, helping seniors, gardening, playing music, working at animal shelters, creating art. The list is as varied as the number of people on this planet. At first, most people have no idea what they would do if time and money were no object. If you're drawing a blank, don't despair. Just remember that in today's busy world, we tend to spend more time thinking of what we *have* to do versus what we *love* to do!

Part B.
Now write down your talents. Don't be modest! We all have amazing talents. What are your strengths? What are your talents? This is the exercise where most people come up short with answers. *Monkey Mind* is probably telling you that this exercise is a waste of time and that there are not many things you're good at, or that you can never earn money doing the things you love. One woman I know told me she knew she was destined to be a writer when she was nine years old, but went into other professions because her family and school advisors told her she could never make a living putting words on paper. A few decades later, after a series of "downsizing" layoffs, she started a business writing service which continues to provide a fine income and satisfies her creative desires – doing the thing she loves the most.

Pick up your pen and write down all that comes to mind. Consider this a private brag session. Giving personal recognition to your talents and strengths allows others to see them as well.

Part C.
Now compare the two lists and come up with some jobs that match what you love with your talents. You may need to do some research as some jobs aren't necessarily common – but they're out there. People get paid for the craziest things – think about professional shoppers, or the travel enthusiasts who earn money while traveling by being a courier. With credit card debt or a family to support, you may not be in a posi-

tion to change jobs right now, but isn't it at least worth exploring? The 40-plus hours a week that most of us spend working is precious and an integral part of our lives. *And it should be questioned.* Remember – if you decide that now is not the time to make a change due to practical reasons, just make sure that you enjoy the time you spend outside the workplace. When you utilize your talents and strengths and when you're doing things you love to do, your spirit will be nurtured and you will automatically feel more energized. If your current line of work is not your *ideal* occupation, know that this can be a temporary situation – *if you choose*. By exploring activities outside of work that bring you joy and express who you really are, an uncomfortable or unfulfilling work situation can be made more palatable and you may even create future opportunities for yourself.

I was a mortgage broker for many years. I was good at my job, but there came a time when I was no longer fulfilled. I loved the fact that it was in the area of finance, but it became routine and mundane, I wasn't challenged and I wasn't willing to continue in that particular line of work. It became a J.O.B. for me and I found myself in my *comfort zone*, knowing I wasn't happy but afraid to make the change. *Monkey Mind* was telling me that this was all I knew how to do and it would be foolish to pursue any new avenues.

When I did the exercise I've just asked you to do, I realized that I loved public speaking and sharing knowledge to help people become more fulfilled in their lives. My strengths are inspiring others and teaching in ways that make learning easy and lots of fun. I started leading homebuyer seminars to help people realize their dream of purchasing a home. They were very popular – and joy was brought back into my work. Ultimately, out of this process, The Debt Free Diva was born! By reconnecting with my strengths and talents and letting myself shine through what I love to do, I brought a sense of purpose into my life. Had I not followed my passion and starting leading the seminars, I may not have discovered my calling in life! Success is infectious and as we exhibit the courage to pursue our dreams and passions, more is given to us.

What's calling YOU?

WORKING WITH REALITY
There are always parts of our job that are unpleasant or could be improved – even for those of us who are really passionate at work. Those of you who really don't like your job can probably find ways to improve your situation until you can find something better. Take a few moments and describe your work. List three things that you love about it and three things that would benefit from improvement. If you can't find three things you love, are there three things you like or appreciate? You may appreciate that the office is close to home, or that your co-workers are kind or that the air conditioning works on a hot summer day. I know you can come up with at least three!

What I love, like or appreciate...
1)
2)
3)

What could be improved...
1)
2)
3)

Consider what you love about your job. When we realign ourselves with what we *do* enjoy about our work, it puts things back into perspective. What might you be able to contribute at work that brings out your talents? When we feel lost in the forest, it's difficult to see the trees, distorting our perception of the situation or event. It also helps to seek out and surround yourself with people who are focused on creating a positive environment.

Now consider the parts of your job that need improvement. Are there resources you could tap to make these parts of your job better? Are you part of the problem or part of the solution?

It's amazing what we can get if we are willing to ask, and I encourage you to think in these terms: Ask for 100% of what you want, 100% of the time. Be willing to hear "no," and open to negotiating a win/win solution. Find the subtle layers of your work – the not-so-visible results of your work. A friend of mine worked part-time at a hospital filing papers while she was going to college. After a couple of days, she knew filing wasn't her life-long passion and was bored stiff. But when she thought of herself as helping doctors keep track of sick patients, she was able to see how her job was making a difference; filing became enjoyable and she prided herself on making sure the medical staff never lost track of a single document. It's important to make the best of what we have and be grateful for our jobs – even if we're looking for new ones! Remember, it's your attitude that will determine the quality of every area of your life.

GOLDEN HANDCUFFS

Do you feel locked into your job and its financial promise as a means to maintaining the lifestyle you want, as if you were wearing *golden handcuffs*? Many people feel this way because they are not willing to walk away from their work. Losing the prestige and security of a consistent paycheck is too much of a sacrifice. Ask yourself the following questions:

- Are you your job, your job description or your income?
- Do you identify yourself solely through your work or through the money that you make?
- If you lost your job would it change who you are?
- If you changed jobs would you be embarrassed or ashamed?

If you answered *yes* to one or more of these questions, rethink your work – or add more balance to your life.

Some of us are on the other side of the spectrum from *golden handcuffs* – needing the work and money just to survive – there's no room to budge and you're just plain *trapped*. The executive who wears *Golden Handcuffs* feels pressured to live in a neighborhood, drive a car and practice a lifestyle commensurate with their earnings, having to make ends meet just as much as the hourly worker at the grocery store.

The interesting thing about money is that it really knows no socioeconomic boundaries. The person earning $20,000 a year with a lot of debt experiences similar emotions to the person earning $200,000 a year who also has a lot of debt. However, the person who earns $20,000 a year while keeping debt in perspective and holding a strong sense of self worth is in a preferable situation to the person earning $200,000 a year who feels they must strive to make more in order to feel better and look good. **It's not a matter of *how much* you earn, it's a matter of** *what you do* with what you earn. There will always be people with more or less money than you. When you have a strong sense of self worth, you'll be less likely to get caught in the *cost of comparison*. The cost of comparison is simply Monkey Mind telling you that you're not good enough until you earn more money and have a more important title. There is honor and dignity in every occupation, from the lowest to the highest – and all are important to the function of our society.

In today's economic climate, there are no guarantees of job security – even more reason to be crystal clear on what's important to you and act on it.

HONORING YOURSELF AT WORK –
BRING A BONUS TO RECEIVE A BONUS

Are you giving your full value at work? We give time and energy to our work – *and*, we receive a paycheck. It's important to honor ourselves no matter where we happen to be working. When you bring a bonus, by putting extra effort into your work, you are likely to be rewarded at work, but you will most definitely be rewarded inside by the increase in self worth and the sense of accomplishment and confidence you will feel by doing your best.

Little things make a big difference. Honoring yourself means not taking advantage of a situation at work – no matter how insignificant something may seem. Using the company phone, email or supplies for personal use may seem trivial and others may make a regular habit of abusing these things. But honoring yourself means honoring your employer. When we use the company phone for personal use, or bring paper clips and envelopes home with us, we're really *leaking* energy. Oprah Winfrey says, "We are what we believe." And if we believe we are a valued employee, providing our employer with a valuable service, we will *be* valued. The golden rule applies in your employment as well as your personal relationships – treat your employer as you would like to be treated. If you don't like your job or aren't being treated fairly, you have the responsibility to get out!

You owe it to yourself to be in tune with the work that you do, for it is the gift that you share with the world. If you're spending five days a week immersed in this work, you deserve to look forward to it with

anticipation, and be constantly contributing and learning. Finally, it's important to distinguish between different levels of work:
- A JOB is something you do to pay the bills. It doesn't always ignite your passions but it serves an important purpose. This is the category where we are most likely to get trapped.
Characteristics: Survival and lack of joy
- A CAREER is a line of work with a destination in mind. It often takes years to build, has ups and downs, but creates a great sense of satisfaction. It takes commitment and persistence and the climb to the top can involve many sacrifices if not kept in balance. A career sometimes comes with important titles, and nice salaries. It not only pays the bills, it builds for the future.
Characteristics: Building for the future, in pursuit of success, structured journey
- A VOCATION is a *calling*. This is work that you know you were born to do. You can feel it in every cell of your body and often like a career, it can consume your time and energy. A vocation carries with it the purpose of healing the world in some fashion utilizing your own strengths and talents. It brings great fulfillment and interestingly is not always associated with making large sums of money. Usually people following their vocation are not focused on money for accumulation sake, more for the quality of work they are doing and the purpose being served. In many cases, the money flows as a natural by-product.
Characteristics: Having a vision, sense of contribution, creating a legacy

What really matters in work is that your emotional and financial needs are being met, and that you feel a high level of esteem in what you do. Given that we spend the majority of each day at our work, it's important that we feel positively balanced and energized to handle all situations that come our way.

CHAPTER 14
CHANGE OF SCENERY

"Feel the fear and do it anyway."

Susan Jeffers

CHAPTER 14 • CHANGE OF SCENERY

DIVA SPEAK:
I handle change with flexibility, confidence and ease.

Prospera and her husband, **Prospero**, were good with money, having created a spending plan that worked for both of them. They were both working, and saving for their dream retirement. Everything was moving along as planned, until Prospera became pregnant. The couple was excited about starting a family, but became concerned about finances. All their friends complained about how expensive it was to raise children; Prospera and Prospero wanted to make sure they could stick with their retirement plans, and have the money to support their new addition. Prospera hoped to be able to work part-time after the baby arrived, so she created a proposal that outlined how her work responsibilities would be fulfilled despite the decrease in hours. Her boss was so impressed that she agreed to let Prospera try the part-time arrangement after the baby arrived. The happy couple began immediately to live based on the income Prospera would have *after* the baby was born, and put the rest of her pre-delivery money in their "baby fund." They determined where they could cut back, have continued with their retirement plans and started a college fund. Meanwhile, the boss reports Prospera's work is better than ever!

KEEPING PERSPECTIVE
We go through many changes in our lifetimes. Whether the situations listed below apply to you or not, they have a common thread – money.

We anticipate or plan for some changes, while others come as a complete surprise. We must learn to keep change in perspective, and aligned with our values. If need be, refer back to Chapter 3 to reconnect with what you value most in your life. *Keeping it in perspective* means bringing simplicity to a complex situation. No matter what your situation is, you are not alone – others are going through the same thing. When you feel you need a helping hand or just someone to talk to, don't be afraid to reach out. With the help of the Internet, it's easier now than ever before!

BOUNCING BABIES
A new baby in the home brings about so many different emotions – it's easy to be frightened *and* joyful within the space of 30 seconds! A new addition can put a strain on your financial life, but if you've planed ahead as much as possible, you can keep your financial life in check. For those couples who plan to have one parent stay at home after the birth, try living on one income during pregnancy to see what changes you will need to make in your spending. And if both parents are planning to continue working, add up all the costs associated with your choice – daycare, commuting, clothes, dry-cleaning. You may find that it is more costly to maintain two incomes than to live on one when all the extra expenses are factored in. Many women have decided to stay home with their kids, finding part-time work that they can do at the kitchen table or in a home office. The explosion of telecommuting positions available through today's technology has opened a plethora of options. Just remember that the *SuperMom* syndrome, trying to do it all and be it all – is a sure fire way to burn yourself out in no time flat. Take the time to determine what is most important to you and stick with that.

KIDS AND COLLEGE
If you've decided to help your children pay for college – the earlier you can start putting money aside the better off you'll be. Even though you may be convinced that your two-year old will have no problem getting a scholarship, it's important to plan ahead! With the costs of education rising faster than inflation, you can try and estimate how much you'll need when your child is ready. There are many web-sites available that can help you determine how much to put away every month. With Education IRA's and 529 plans available, you can also take advantage of

tax breaks for money that will be used for higher education. As with all aspects of your money life, preplanning and taking action are the keys.

SANDWICH GENERATION

Having children later in life has become commonplace, putting many parents in the "sandwich generation," taking care of young kids and aging parents at the same time. Although it's impossible to predict the future, it can be an expensive endeavor and one that deserves serious consideration. All the more reason to address your financial situation if you know this scenario will become a reality for you in the near future or down the road. Some areas to consider are daycare, extended care, health care and sources of income that are and will be available. It will probably be stressful if you don't take the necessary steps ahead of time. Often, it can be overwhelming and sometimes depressing to think about these areas and the potential costs involved, however, it's the act of pre-planning that can relieve feeling overwhelmed and stressed.

SABBATICALS

Just a generation ago, many Americans stayed with the same company for 40 years, got a gold watch and began retirement. What a different working environment we are in today! As we change jobs and switch careers much more frequently now, many of us have the opportunity to take a sabbatical. People take sabbaticals for all sorts of reasons – to contemplate a career switch, to spend time with family, to travel the world, to volunteer or to simply take a break. Again, there are entire books on sabbaticals and how to plan for them, but here are a few questions you'll need to ask yourself if it sounds interesting to you:

1) Is this feasible in the context of my other plans?
2) Will I make any money on my sabbatical?
3) How much additional money will I need?
4) What do I hope to gain personally?
5) What will I do when I finish my sabbatical?

Again, thoughtful pre-planning is what will be required if you hope to take a sabbatical.

50'S, 60'S AND BEYOND

Retirement looks very different today than in previous generations. Today, people can retire "early," or chose to not retire at all. They're making career changes, or volunteering for a favorite cause. They're working part-time or simply taking it easy for a while. There are no retirement rules and it's fun to dream! With this scenario comes a lot of financial concerns and questions of self worth. *What will I do with the rest of my life? Will I have the money I need to live comfortably? It's been a long time since I've done anything else – will I know what to do?* It's so important to be prepared with a concrete plan in place rather than make a spontaneous change.

INSTANT INHERITORS

Winning millions in a lottery or receiving a surprise inheritance from a long lost uncle may seem like the answer to our prayers – but the truth is that there are challenges and responsibilities that come with the sudden receipt of a large sum of money. If we had bad spending habits to begin with, we can easily blow through the money and even get back into debt! If we're also grieving the loss of a loved one, there are added emotions – and dealing with the money is probably not high on our list of priorities. My first recommendation is to put the money into a money market account and just leave it alone for a while. If you have debts that need to be paid, pay them, but don't spend anything until you've had some time to think. Take a couple of weeks and go back through the exercises you've completed in this book. Really think about what matters to you and keep your plan simple.

SUDDENLY SINGLE

Becoming suddenly single is probably not something that we necessarily plan, but there are things we can do – single or married – that can keep us protected. First, always keep a checking account in your name. Even if you have joint accounts, it's important to establish your own credit with an additional account of your own. The same goes for a credit card – keep one in your name. It's also crucial to be aware of debt that your partner may be carrying, as you may be responsible for paying back that debt – depending on where you live and other circumstances. We're back to the key to good relationships with others involving money – good communication!

MR. MOM – THE STAY-AT-HOME DAD

More men are staying home with the kids than ever before as women have become so predominant and powerful in today's workforce. Typically when a change occurs in society, there is a space before the change is embraced by the mainstream. If your husband is a stay-at-home dad and it works for your family then forget what society may be telling you. The reality is that women have strong earning capacities now and for many families it makes perfect financial sense for dad to stay at home. Or perhaps dad is better suited to take care of the children. You may actually be getting grief from others for simply doing what you think is best. Ignore them and think of yourselves as being part of a revolution!

ONE MAMA, TWO DADDIES, THREE PARENTS... OR FOUR
Roughly half the children in America today grow up in a single-parent home, or with step-parents. Whatever the situation is in your family, as parents you are responsible for giving the children in your home a consistent message about money. Set up a meeting with everyone who has parenting responsibilities for your child and discuss some things that you all agree would be beneficial for the child when it comes to money – allowances, working for extra money, how the child should spend and save, etc. It may not be easy, but if you can make it work it's a tremendous gift you can give your child for his or her future. Determine ahead of time which parent will be responsible for certain expenses and do your very best to make sure your children aren't getting caught in the middle. Cherish and respect them enough to help them build a healthy emotional and practical relationship to money.

JUST OUT OF A JOB
We never really *expect* to be out of a job, but if it happens to you, take some time to regroup. Do things that will make you feel better about yourself and think about what is really important to you. Consider the stages you'll go through, and know that this situation is temporary.
  Stage 1: Denial
  Stage 2: Anger
  Stage 3: Acceptance

  We begin to get ourselves back on track by finding a new job, creating an entirely new career, or taking an early retirement in Stage 3 – acceptance.

COLLEGE TO REAL WORLD
We're legally adults at age 18, but for many of us the "real world" hits us when we graduate from college and get a "real job." During college,

many of us became quite adept at using credit cards. As I mentioned earlier, colleges and universities all over the country are *compensated* by the credit card companies for letting them market to students and faculty. For many students, their first lessons in money management come in the form of outrageous bills from credit card companies. In college and after graduation, many of us are burdened not only with student loans, but with massive debt as well. It's common during college to think, "I'll pay this off when I'm making *real money* – after I graduate." Unfortunately, many jobs right out of college don't pay big bucks, so it's a struggle to be in the adult world for the first time with credit card debt and student loans hovering over your head. If you're in this position, take a moment and congratulate yourself. Go ahead and pat yourself on the back. (I really want you to stop and do it!) You've graduated with a degree and it's a terrific investment for your future.

As you ponder how you're going to get the debt monkey off your back, look at the situation objectively and calmly. Most student loans have low interest rates, so concentrate on paying the higher-interest credit cards first. Go back through the chapter on debt and set up a systematic approach to paying it off. And don't fall into the trap that many recent graduates do: They tell themselves they'll pay it off when they get a higher paying job or that next promotion. Work on paying it off now even if the process is moving slowly. When you get the higher paying job or a promotion, you'll be that much closer to having your debt gone for good, and that much closer to living your dream.

DEBT-FREE DIVA CPR

Here's my life-saving technique for times of financial crisis:

Communicate – when you can't pay your bills, communicate with creditors and make sure they are aware of your situation. Many times, a mutual agreement can be met that works for both parties.

Prioritize – If you need to pare down and minimize some expenses, here is where you can start to determine what you really need to get you through this transition. In addition to determining between *needs* and *wants*, it's important to be clear on what you *can't* or *won't* do.

Restructure – Create a new routine for your day. Create whatever works for you, but this is what I recommend to those that need some guidance:

1) Set aside part of the day to feel "blah." Place a time limit by telling yourself, "I can lie around and feel sorry for myself from 9:00 – 9:30 and then I'm moving on with my day."
2) Set aside part of the day to "get results." This time is dedicate to doing at least one thing that will move you closer to what you want – update your resume, or make job-related phone calls.
3) Set aside part of the day for a time of rejuvenation – but make sure that it comes *after* your results period! Spend this time exercising, meditating or doing whatever you need to feel good.

When you take the time to restructure your routine, it puts *you* in control. And control is a great thing to have when you're out-of-work and feeling vulnerable.

CHAPTER 15

LIVE THE DREAM

"Follow your bliss."

Joseph Campbell

CHAPTER 15 • LIVE THE DREAM

Congratulations! You've done great work! Savor each step you've taken toward living your dream and reinventing your relationship to money. Check in to review the work you've done as often as needed. And remember the saying: *Use it or Lose It*. Your new and improved relationship to money will depend on your being willing to stick to your plan – with E.A.S.E:

Education, **A**ction, **S**upport, **E**nergize
I cannot emphasize enough how important it is for you to continue following this formula for the creation of your dreams. Each component is dependent on the others, so be sure to integrate them all. They'll soon become a familiar part of your life, if they haven't already.

DIVA SPEAK:
I've compiled all the DIVA SPEAK affirmations here in the final chapter for a good reason. I recommend that you say them aloud three times every day, and write them once every day for the next 21 days. This isn't meant to add more work to your day – it will make a difference in your life, causing you to hold a mindset of abundance and prosperity. Scientific studies prove that it takes 21 days of consistent repetition for a thought or process to become a neuronal pathway – an automatic thought or process recorded in our brain tissue. I learned of this technique from master prosperity teacher Edwene Gaines; I practiced it for 21 days and was amazed at the unexpected surprises that came into my life. I didn't win the lottery, but I noticed so many little things that have made such a big difference in my life. Remember, write them once and speak

them aloud three times with feeling, every day for 21 days, starting today. Feel the words as you speak them and create a warm glow within, as you become a *Debt Free Diva!*

1) I am open to telling the truth about my current relationship to money so that I can take positive steps.
2) I am willing to see my relationship to money from a new perspective – my *true* perspective.
3) I am my own dream weaver.
4) I am willing to track my expenses and record my progress *with ease* for the next 90 days.
5) I am capable of attaining my money goals with E.A.S.E.
6) I have all the time and money I need to feel secure and live my dreams.
7) I am abundant in my self worth *and* my net worth.
8) I handle my money with E.A.S.E and always have money available.
9) I am responsible with my debt and keep it in perspective.
10) I am open and receptive to learning about investing for my future with E.A.S.E.
11) I am the *CEO* of my financial life, focused on *Creating Extraordinary Outcomes.*
12) I am always clear and concise in my communication about money.
13) I am open to creating a work environment that honors who I am.
14) I handle change with flexibility, confidence and ease.
15) I am an incredible Debt Free Diva!

EXPECTATIONS

Our expectations, whether they be positive or negative, determine how we move forward in our relationship to money. Are you familiar with the saying *"If you don't set your sights too high, you won't get disappointed"?* So many people feel that having positive expectations is a setup for failure and disappointment. I tell you this is not true – it's holding *unrealistic* expectations that set us up for failure and disappointment. For me, that was the expectation of earning $250,000 and buying a brand new BMW in my first year of a commission sales job! Since I didn't make it I felt terrible about myself. In retrospect, it was an extremely *unrealistic expectation*. There's a lot of wisdom in setting realistic goals and taking baby steps to get there. It's with each successive baby step that monumental progress is made.

Patience is a key ingredient in meeting our expectations. It's hard to be patient – we live in a culture given to instant gratification, we want things to happen for us with the snap of a finger. Patience allows us to learn life's lessons along the way, and to remember that the journey is actually more important than arriving at your goal. The Buddhists say the journey *is* the goal. I've spoken to many successful people in my life and they've unanimously shared that in addition to a feeling of fulfillment upon reaching a desired goal, there was also a feeling of *what's next*?

Your last assignment in this book is to write down *your* financial expectations for the next six months. Include what is realistic for you. This requires that you *tell the truth* about where you are and set your sights on where you want to be. Six months will pass quickly, so set baby steps for yourself. For example, you may want to have an investment account balance of $300 in the next 6 months. In order to make it happen you may have to open a money market account and every month for the next 6 months, deposit $50 into that account. It's very important to be specific so that you will know exactly what action you need to take. If you were to simply write down that you will have an investment account started in the next 6 months, that becomes an open invitation to take no action at all. Also, *Monkey Mind* will no doubt tell you that what you're setting out to do is meaningless or not ambitious enough, and to not bother doing it at all. Thank *Monkey Mind* for sharing, and carry on with defining your financial expectations!

Make a copy of your list and email it to **coach@debtfreediva.com**

Sending them to me creates accountability. Although you're reinventing your relationship to money for yourself and your family, when someone else is expecting and rooting for your success, their support aids your individual efforts. Contrary to popular belief, it's almost impossible to make any positive and lasting change *by yourself*. It may be quite valiant to think that you can, but where two or more minds are gathered, positive change comes about with greater ease. While writing this book for you, I have had a team of supporters holding me accountable and cheering me on. But I first had to tell them what I expected for the book – content, chapters and timelines. If I had attempted to create this book for you *all by my lonesome*, chances are high that it would have taken far longer to complete!

Now take the original and seal it in an envelope. Mark the date six months from today on the outside of the envelope and set it aside to open on that date. Mark the date in your planner or Palm Pilot with countdown reminders each month.

The first time I did this exercise, I wrote down one expectation I had for each area of my life. I sealed it in an envelope and put it away and literally forgot about it. But I had no action plan that would take me step by step toward my goal. What was really interesting was that when I opened the envelope six months later, I was amazed to see what I had accomplished with relative ease! Also interesting was the fact that the things I did not complete were things that were either unrealistic to attain in a six-month period, or they simply weren't important to me. That is why I ask you to write an action plan consisting of attainable baby steps.

The final note I have to share on *expectations* is that it is imperative that you *expect the best* for yourself. I mean this sincerely because if you can't be your own best fan, how can you expect others to be? Often people associate expecting the best for themselves as arrogant, as less than humble. I believe it's quite the opposite. I believe that most of us have spent far too much time *not* believing in ourselves and not expecting the very best life has to offer. It's time to forgive yourself and others for past mistakes, look to your future with abundant joy and hope, and to wish the same for others. Creating your dream life takes place in the present moment – and each moment is the present moment. Remember I shared with you that what you think about, you talk about and what you talk about you bring about? Your thoughts, your intentions, your words and your actions shape your life. The best news is that you have *choice* and are, therefore, in full control. You know where you are, you know where you're going and I believe that in each moment you will know what you need to do and most importantly, who you need to be. You are an *amazing diva*, and it's time for you to live the life you always dreamed of – *emotionally, financially, physically and spiritually!*

THE LAW OF GIVING AND RECEIVING

The last thing you may be thinking about – especially when you're in debt – is giving to others. But the truth is, when we get in the habit of both giving and receiving the world opens up immense possibilities to us. When you're feeling stressed and overwhelmed about finances, the first thing to do is look around and give to someone in need. When you give from your heart with no expectation to receive, you will be pleasantly surprised at what will be in store for you. Give often of your money, love and time. How much we give and where we give is our own agreement with the universe – there are no set rules. But whatever it is we are lacking – that's what we need to give first. I'm sure you've heard the phrase "In order to *have* a friend you have to first *be* a friend." When you are secure within yourself and have a positive relationship to money, it makes it much easier and you will automatically be willing to give back. Start small, and start now.

My first experiences of giving were *white-knucklers!* Monkey Mind was screaming – telling me I couldn't really spare this money, I should wait until I had more money for myself before I started giving. I had a huge debate going on in my mind and literally everything around me became silent as the voice inside me grew louder. I was afraid to give for fear that I wouldn't have enough for myself. Nevertheless, I gave $50 dollars to someone in need, and carried on. Each time, the giving became easier. Occasionally, the fear would creep in but I continued to give. What I discovered over time was that money seemed to flow more easily in and out of my life. I was no longer focused on not having enough. A few times, money came *to me* when I least expected it. What I had developed through giving was the belief that I was able to share my resources – that was my way of affirming that I had abundance in my life and would never go without.

The fear that I may not have enough still creeps back into my life from time to time, even now! But when I take the time to get back to the present moment, take some deep breaths and affirm that I have everything that I need, I gain perspective on what's truly important to me and I can move on with belief and confidence. You can give of your time, your money and your talents. If you feel lack in your life, I guarantee that through the grace of giving, you will feel abundance like you've never felt before.

It's actually harder for most people to receive than it is to give. Why is this so? When you are giving to someone, you are being appreciated and validated which increases your self-worth. When we receive, it can bring up fears around not being worthy and deserving, or a belief that now we *owe* them. I have a dear friend who is the consummate giver – kind, generous and readily available to lend a hand always. However, when it comes to receiving, she feels uncomfortable since she is supposed to be quite capable of being independent and self-sufficient. She feels uneasy when people give to her or do things for her. We've discussed this many times and step by step she is allowing in love and support. It's a fear of not being good enough, it's a lack of self-esteem, it's a fear of being vulnerable to others. If receiving is hard for you, I ask you to consider the following: *What does it feel like when you do something for someone else?* Wouldn't it be wonderful if someone else could feel that way by doing something for you?

Culturally, we yearn for connection, but shut it out in many ways. We must practice the law of giving and receiving within our personal communities if we wish to foster an environment of prosperity and goodwill. In the broadest sense, the money that flows through our lives is not *really* ours – but a part of our universe. Let's be good stewards of it.

NINE STEPS FOR LIVING YOUR DREAMS

We've been through a lot in this book and hopefully you've begun to make progress toward living your dreams. There will be frustrating times, and some things will come easier than others. When you feel yourself slipping back into your old ways, consider the following:

9 Steps for Living Your Dreams

1) Admit that you need help.
2) Be open and willing to change. When you decide what you're willing to do, your life will move forward. Being willing brings about a commitment to experience everything involved in making a change.
3) Discern the difference between what you *can* do and what you *will* do. If you need to lose weight and you post a picture of yourself naked, you *will* work out!
4) Use the E.A.S.E. formula for developing new skills

5) In the next 24 hours, take what you've learned and teach it. When you teach it, you learn it. When you give it away, it comes back to you tenfold.
6) When you learn something new – review, review, review. Remember, it takes repeating something at least 21 times before it becomes a habit and a way of life.
7) Be grateful for all that you have and know that you *always* have enough.
8) Be proactive – not reactive. It's a guarantee that as soon as you learn something new, life will hit you at 100 mph. Your ability to get back on track will depend on the importance you place on your life from this day forward.
9) Celebrate your successes. By taking the time to celebrate, we avoid feeling that we should *always* be doing more – we get in tune with what we have to be grateful for in the present moment.

I wish you all the best as you continue your journey of reinventing your relationship to money and living your dreams. I'd like to close with lyrics from one of my favorite songs, "I Hope You Dance," written by Mark D. Sanders and Tia Sillers and sung by LeeAnn Womack:

I hope you still feel small when you stand beside the ocean
And whenever one door closes, I hope one more opens
Promise me that you'll give faith a fighting chance
And when you get the choice to sit it out or dance
I hope you dance...

May you forever be blessed with all the time, the courage and the money to live your dreams...

ACKNOWLEDGEMENTS

The creation of "The Debt Free Diva – From Self Worth to Net Worth" has been an amazing journey, full of every emotion imaginable. Without the constant and loyal support of my incredible Diva team, this work would have been much longer in the making. Through the countless gifts of unconditional love, I learned what it was like to have people be there and believe in me more than I could at times for myself. There were many moments when my creative flow was challenged and there was *always* a friend on hand to remind me of my vision and purpose for writing this book. My gratitude runs deep within my heart for the incredible spirits I have been touched by.

I believe that people come into our lives at different times and *always* for a reason. Some stay for a short time while others create a lasting presence.

To Judith Shaver, you have seen me through *everything* and been the most steadfast influence in my life. My love and thanks for being my biggest fan!

To Lisa Lapides - Sawicki, my "beyond" superstar publicist! You have been my breath of fresh air since we met and I can honestly say that I believe more in myself today as a result of having met you. You have created a place where I have been able to celebrate, seek solace, vent, laugh, cry and above all, come home to. The spirit of love that you are allows for infant dreams to become reality.

To Cathy Lamar, coach extraordinaire! You reminded me that my brilliance is ignited from within. In every moment, you've been there with the inspiration and encouragement that I needed to take my next step.

To Lesley Wright, your creative talents brought to The Debt Free Diva a depth of timeless wisdom. Thank you for your incredible branding and for showing me how my heritage gives me wings to fly.

To my editors Laurie Dunn and Linda Anger, thank you for your incredible mastery with words. You were able to help me take the pictures and words from my mind to paint the canvas before me. An editors job is complex and you are both brilliant at your craft.

My heartfelt thanks, to my dear friends in Detroit, Toronto and Vancouver who have nurtured me throughout this process. You all know who you are and you have been amazing cheerleaders! A special acknowledgment to Marianne Williamson whose lessons instilled in me the courage, commitment and faith to follow my dreams. You are all truly amazing spirits!

And finally, to my loving parents, Vera and Bruce. Thank you for having me believe that whatever I set out to do is always within my reach. I am so grateful for everything you have done for me. I love you with all my heart.

Dee Dee Sung
2003

NOTES

NOTES